Restoring Christian Modesty

© 2019 Jesse Smith

Restoring Christian Modesty
God's Perfect Will for Your Outward Appearance

First Edition, January 2019

Published by

BRIDE OF CHRIST MINISTRIES

Publishing and Design Services: Melinda Martin, MelindaMartin.me

Restoring Christian Modesty: God's Perfect Will for Your Outward Appearance is under copyright protection. No part of this book may be used or reproduced in any manner whatsoever without written permission except in the case of brief quotations embodied in critical articles and reviews. Printed in the United States of America. All rights reserved.

Scripture quotations from The Authorized (King James) Version. Rights in the Authorized Version in the United Kingdom are vested in the Crown. Reproduced by permission of the Crown's patentee, Cambridge University Press.

ISBN: 978-1-7336649-0-5 (paperback), 978-1-7336649-1-2 (epub)

Restoring Christian Modesty

God's Perfect Will for Your Outward Appearance

Jesse Smith

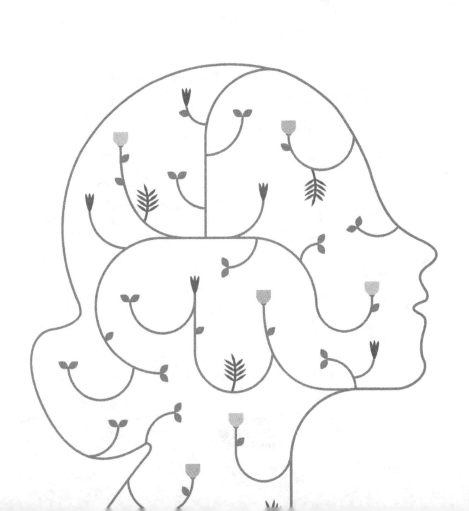

Restoring Christian Modesty

CONTENTS

Introduction 1

Chapter 1: A Biblical Foundation for Your Outward Appearance 3

Chapter 2: How to Apply Old Testament Scripture to the New Testament . 21

Chapter 3: The Four Guidelines for Modest Clothing 41

Chapter 4: Hair Length 57

Chapter 5: Jewelry, Makeup, Tattoos, and High Heels 67

Chapter 6: Connecting American Fashion History with the Bible 85

Chapter 7: YouTube Testimonies, Questions and Answers 107

Chapter 8: The Perfect Will of God 123

Works Cited 141

About the Author 147

INTRODUCTION

"Are long dresses part of your religion? I see all of your daughters are wearing them," a sales associate asked me recently.

I was so happy to receive her respectful question about our personal convictions. "Yes, we believe men and women should wear separate garments as God taught Israel in Deuteronomy 22:5."

Thinking on this exchange, I really appreciated the manner in which this person asked about our clothing choices. In my 16 years of following the Bible's standard of separate garments for men and women, I have had very few people ask why I hold this conviction. Most people, including myself and my own family and friends, seem to be uncomfortable addressing others' faith-based convictions, especially out in public.

Not long after this friendly encounter, I felt a great burden to write this book so I could clearly and fully explain what God's Word teaches about a modest outward appearance.

I have approached this book in the same manner as the sales associate approached me—with kindness and respect. I realize that most people have been raised unaware of God's standards for a sanctified life. When a person watches one of my teaching videos on YouTube or reads this book, it is likely that he or she is hearing this truth of God for the first time. Therefore, I take the responsibility of presenting God's unchanging truth very seriously.

If you can receive God's requirements for holiness as taught in this book, major changes will certainly take place in your life. The changes will not be as difficult if you can sense the goodness of God that has brought you to the knowledge of holiness, for it is God's goodness that leads us to repentance.[1]

I want to present God's standards for our outward appearance with a Biblical and historical foundation so you have assurance of the perfect will of God for

---

1   *The Holy Bible,* Romans 2:4

your life. Jesus is the Word of God and our Rock.[2] When you believe God's words about living a holy life and apply them to your life, you can be certain you are pleasing God and building your life upon the Rock—the eternal, infallible, unchanging Word of God.[3]

Keep your Bible handy as you read through this book, as I will reference hundreds of Scriptures. You will be delighted to read with your own eyes all that God's Word teaches about this subject.

I desire that you'll know and obey God's perfect will for your outward appearance at the conclusion of this book. May you be a willing participant in God's restoration of Christian modesty.

I plan to revisit the sales associate so I can hand her a free copy of the finished book you are holding in your hands.

---

2 John 1:1-14, 1 Corinthians 10:4
3 Matthew 7:24

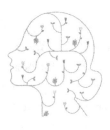

CHAPTER 1

A Biblical Foundation for Your Outward Appearance

"But as he which hath called you is holy, so be ye holy in all manner of conversation;"

—1 Peter 1:15

The Word of God is Our Foundation

The Biblical foundation for the doctrine of holiness in appearance begins with the Word of God, forever settled in heaven.[4] It is so enduring that heaven and earth will pass away while God's Words can never pass away.[5] Jesus Christ taught that every detail of the Word would be fulfilled.[6]

Scriptural knowledge makes us wise unto salvation and is profitable for doctrine, reproof, correction, and instruction in righteousness.[7] When we read the Bible with a hungry heart, the Holy Spirit reveals God's perfect will for every area of our lives, even our outward appearance.

The Word delivers a standard of truth that transcends ages, generations and societies because God's holy nature is always the same and does not change.[8] God's standards, or rules, for outward appearance have remained unchanged

---

4   Psalm 119:89
5   Matthew 24:35
6   Matthew 5:18
7   2 Timothy 3:15-16
8   Psalm 102:24-27, Malachi 3:6, Hebrews 1:12, 13:8

from Genesis 3:21 to Revelation 22:21. You and I can have confidence that this standard is the same today as it was for Adam and Eve.

The New Testament gospel that Christ gave to Paul will be used to judge the secrets of men's hearts on the day of judgment.[9] Humanity will not be judged by any denomination's understanding, but rather by God's own revelation of His Word. Since the Word of God is the standard for judgment, you must diligently seek God until He reveals this true interpretation of the Bible to your heart.

You must also apply the many thoughts in the Bible correctly to your life. Recall that even Satan quoted the Word of God to Jesus at His three temptations in the wilderness, but Satan's applications were always rooted in idolatry, unbelief, or pride.[10] You should study every word in the Bible and pray for God's understanding of Scripture and its application to your life.

THE RIGHTLY DIVIDED WORD OF TRUTH

The Savior taught that you are to live by every Word that proceeds out of the mouth of God.[11] If you must live by every Word of God, you must know how portions of Scripture pertain to you. Thankfully, God promised to send men who were gifted with five different, but complementary, preaching gifts to bring unity to the faith and bring believers to a state of spiritual completion.[12] Additionally, Paul stated that gifted preachers would be able to rightly divide God's Word to His people.[13] True gospel preaching and teaching will save the preacher and those that believe him.[14]

I pray that the Lord Jesus would use my teaching gift to rightly divide God's truth to you in this often misunderstood area of outward appearance. I am simply teaching what the Holy Spirit has taught me privately and what faithful men have taught me over the years in accordance with 2 Timothy 2:2, *"And the things that thou hast heard of me among many witnesses, the same commit thou to faithful men, who shall be able to teach others also."*

---

9 Romans 2:16, Galatians 1:12
10 Matthew 4:1-11
11 Matthew 4:4
12 Ephesians 4:8-16
13 2 Timothy 2:15
14 1 Timothy 4:16

Knowing the rightly-divided Word of God isn't enough. We need obedience to it. In Matthew 7:24-29, our Lord Jesus taught that obedience to the Word of God is the foundation on which our lives should rest. Those who do the commands of God will have a life able to withstand any trial. In contrast, Jesus then revealed that those who disobey God's Word are in danger of falling from truth when the storms come.

THE PREDICTED FALLING AWAY

The Bible actually predicted a global falling away from obedience to the Word of God before the antichrist would be revealed in the end days.[15] Other portions of Scripture support this prophecy that obedience to the Word of God would continually decrease and obedient Christians would become a very small minority.[16]

Based upon these prophecies, you would expect the majority of those claiming to be Christians would not honor God's Word in many areas of Biblical doctrine, but would fall away from the truth of the Bible in relation to modest clothing, holiness in appearance, and hair length, among other things.

You cannot call your Creator "Lord" if you do not obey His Word, though there are many who will honor God with their lips and yet their hearts will be far from Him.[17] Run from that group and join the faithful, obedient, and diligent followers of the Holy Scripture. Our Lord Jesus Christ asked a very pointed question in Luke 6:46 that you must also ask yourself today, *"And why call ye me, Lord, Lord, and do not the things which I say?"* Your heart should answer this question by saying, "Dear Jesus, my obedience to Your commands proves You are truly my Lord."

WHAT IS HOLINESS?

A life of holiness is a state of constant obedience to God's Word. The Greek Lexicon describes holiness as "consecration, purification, sanctification of heart

---

15   2 Thessalonians 2:3
16   Matthew 7:14, 24:12, 22, Luke 18:8, 2 Timothy 3:1, 13
17   Matthew 7:21-23, Matthew 15:8

and life."[18] Scripture describes a holy life as living without any sin or filthiness in body and mind.[19] Your calling from God is to perfect holiness in reverential fear or respect of Almighty God. In broad terms, holiness includes every action in life.

The focus of this book is conforming your outward appearance to God's standard for holiness. Chapter 3 covers God's four guidelines for modest clothing. Chapter 4 teaches you how long hair should be if you want to live a life of holiness unto God. Chapter 5 examines whether makeup, tattoos, jewelry, high heels, and earrings are holy in the sight of God.

GOD REQUIRES HOLINESS

God requires His New Testament followers to be holy, or set apart from sinful behaviors and lifestyles. Our entire lives should be wholly devoted to serving and pleasing our God. Scripture literally states our purpose: "*That we should be holy and without blame before Him.*"[20]

Our God required holiness, or a separated lifestyle, in the Old Testament and also requires it today in the New Testament. 1 Peter 1:15-16 instructs us to be holy in all manner of "*conversation,*" which in the Greek means "manner of life, conduct, and behavior."[21] Peter was quoting the Old Testament Scriptures from Leviticus 11:44-45 and 20:7 making us aware that many of God's principles of the Old Testament are still in effect today. Chapter 2 explores this concept in depth.

God requires holiness because He purchased us with the precious blood of His Son, Jesus Christ.[22] He is the God of the living and dead and earned the right to be Lord, or ruler, over every soul through the sacrifice of His Son on the cross of Calvary.[23] Paul said we are holy temples or tabernacles. If you will not submit to your Creator and become holy, God will destroy you.[24]

---

18   *Voice of God Recordings Inc.*, "The Bible: Hebrew and Greek Lexicons," www.branham.org/en/messagesearch
19   2 Corinthians 7:1
20   Ephesians 1:4
21   *Voice of God Recordings Inc.*, "The Bible: Hebrew and Greek Lexicons," www.branham.org/en/messagesearch
22   1 Corinthians 6:20, 7:23, 1 Peter 1:18-19
23   Romans 14:7-9
24   1 Corinthians 3:16-17

Living a holy life is an important issue and should be on the minds of anyone serious about loving and serving a holy God. Every man and woman has been given a conscience for the purpose of moral perception, which is to understand if something is right or wrong. When you truly believe in and accept the sacrifice of Jesus Christ in your life, you can now experience a clean, pure conscience that is free from corruption and fully devoted to the service of God.[25] Thereby, you can perceive you are justified from your sins and living right before your Creator.[26]

HOW WE BECOME HOLY

The process of becoming holy or separated from the world is plainly taught in numerous New Testament passages. Paul wrote that Jesus sanctifies and cleanses His church with the washing of water by the Word.[27] Followers of Christ are washed by the Word as they lay apart all filthiness and receive the Word of God.[28] The key to your washing is to voluntarily lay aside all sin and do the will of God.

Peter wrote that we purify our souls through obedience to the Word of God.[29] Obedience can only occur when you die to your own will and do the will of God, as taught by Jesus' submission in Gethsemane.[30] Conversely, a soul that will not obey the Spirit of God is known as subverted, unstable, and ultimately lost.[31]

Being sanctified unto God, completely and wholly, is the absolute will of God for all believers.[32] To do the will of God is God working in us to do His good pleasure.[33] To reject the will of God is to become a worker of iniquity.[34] Without holiness no man shall see the Lord.[35]

---

25 Hebrews 9:14
26 Hebrews 10:2, 22
27 Ephesians 5:25-26
28 James 1:21
29 1 Peter 1:22
30 Mark 14:36
31 Acts 15:24, Titus 3:9-11, 2 Peter 2:14-17
32 2 Corinthians 7:1, 1 Thessalonians 4:3, 5:23
33 Philippians 2:13
34 Matthew 7:21-23
35 Hebrews 12:14

HOLINESS IS BEAUTIFUL

Psalm 96:9 teaches that we should worship the Lord in the beauty of holiness: *"O worship the Lord in the beauty of holiness: fear before him, all the earth."* It is strengthening to know that God sees holy living as beautiful and as an act of true worship.

Hollywood, false religions, and the world will never see God's holiness standards as attractive or beautiful, so we do not expect the world to fall in love with modesty. But we can rest assured that the same God who called us to be holy is the same God who looks down upon His obedient children and sees their character, conduct, and clothing as beautiful in His sight.

Jesus Christ is the very epitome of beauty, not because of His attractive appearance or clothing—but because of His holy, sinless lifestyle and character. Some artists represent Jesus as having an attractive face, shiny hair, and elegant robes, but this idea is completely contrary to Isaiah's description of Christ, when he said *"There is no beauty that we should desire Him."*[36] Jesus' character was beautiful because He always did that which pleased the Father.[37] Christians who live holy have this same attitude, for Paul wrote that we have the same mind of Christ.[38] Your life is beautiful in God's sight when you apply Christ's attitude to your life.

Satan often disguises his temptations by using beauty. Satan's own beauty lifted his heart up in pride against God and led to his being cast out of heaven.[39] Cain tried to offer a more beautiful sacrifice than Abel's, but his offering was rejected.[40] Those who want to appear beautiful to the world's standards today must take heed that they do not repeat the same prideful and devilish mistake as Satan. Promoting your beauty has a strong tendency to lead you away from God's standard of beauty.

Proverbs 31:30 tells us that *"beauty is vain,"* and the most valuable possession we can have is the fear of the Lord, which causes us to hate evil.[41] When you hate evil and abstain from it, you are holy and beautiful in God's sight.

---

36 Isaiah 53:2
37 John 8:29
38 Philippians 2:5
39 Ezekiel 28:11-19
40 Genesis 4:1-16
41 Psalm 111:10, Proverbs 8:13, Ecclesiastes 12:13

LOVE IS THE GREATEST MOTIVATOR

Many people consider standards for holy living as legalism. However, a true understanding of legalism will help you know the difference between an unhealthy, legalistic attitude driven by fear versus a healthy, obedient attitude driven by love. Love is the greatest and only motivation needed for the believer to meet God's requirement for a holy life.

Obedience is accepted by God when love is its motivation. 1 Corinthians chapter 13 teaches that love is the greatest of all gifts. Miracles, knowledge, and understanding all mysteries do not profit believers unless they have the love of God in their hearts as their motivation for every action or work. Love empowers faith, which then produces works.[42] Always obey God in the correct order: love, faith, works.

In St. John chapter 14, the Lord Jesus teaches that love is the only accepted motivation for obedience in the sight of God. In four separate verses, Jesus teaches that love will cause a true believer to keep the commands of God.[43] You are known as a lover of God if you keep the sayings of Jesus.

The earthly life of the Lord Jesus Christ epitomized obeying the commandments of God based upon love. Jesus loved the Father and knew He always pleased Him because He never disobeyed one command despite being tempted in every way.[44] Jesus' love for the Father empowered Him to love His neighbors as Himself, fulfilling all the law of God.[45]

LEGALISM

One definition of legalism is "excessive adherence to law or formula," meaning that the legalist standard is more than necessary.[46] Legalism, then, in Christianity, is adding some requirement to the Bible that God does not require.

There are grave consequences to adding requirements to the Bible. Proverbs says, "*Add thou not unto his words, lest he reprove thee, and thou be found a liar.*"[47]

---

42 Galatians 5:6, James 2:14-16
43 John 14:15, 21, 23, 24
44 John 8:29, 14:31, Hebrews 4:15
45 Galatians 5:14
46 *English Oxford Living Dictionaries,* www.en.oxforddictionaries.com/definition/legalism
47 Proverbs 30:6

Revelation says plagues will be added to those who add to the Book and those who take away will have their heavenly inheritance taken away.[48] God's pure words are sufficient for our complete earthly journey.[49] God's standards for holiness are not legalism, since no requirements have been added to the Bible.

Paul specifically denounced legalism concerning the doctrine of circumcision, teaching that requiring circumcision in the New Testament would be a fall from grace.[50] Paul's encounter with men who taught circumcision was required for salvation led the apostles to have a council about the matter, concluding that Gentiles were not required to be circumcised.[51]

This pattern should be followed today when believers sense a legalistic teaching may be creeping into the Body of Christ. Elders, or leaders of the church, should gather together to pray and search the Scripture in order to provide a clear, concise Biblical answer to the teaching in question. They should also prayerfully seek out wisdom from other seasoned ministers and come to a Bible-based conclusion.

MODESTY

The term "modesty" will show up often in this book and is a command of God. I use this word to focus on the clothing that we wear on our bodies. The context of this term comes from a Scripture about apparel in 1 Timothy 2:9: "*In like manner also, that women adorn themselves in modest apparel, with shamefacedness and sobriety.*" The Greek definition of modesty is "well arranged."[52]

To clarify "modesty," a modern definition is "showing regard for the decencies of behavior, speech, dress."[53] When you dress modestly, you are not drawing attention to your own body. Instead, you redirect attention away from your body by wearing clothes which cover areas of nakedness. Chapter 3 thoroughly explains the four Bible guidelines for covering the parts of the body that God considers nakedness.

---

48 Revelation 22:18-19
49 Proverbs 30:5
50 Galatians 5:1-6, 6:12-15
51 Acts 15:24-29
52 *Voice of God Recordings Inc.*, "The Bible: Hebrew and Greek Lexicons," www.branham.org/en/messagesearch
53 *Dictionary.com*, www.dictionary.com/browse/modest

THE BEGINNING AND ENDING OF MODEST CLOTHING

Genesis, the book of beginnings, is where we see the beginning of modest clothing.

Before their fall into sin, Adam and Eve were both naked and unashamed.[54] Immediately after Eve was deceived into sinning by the serpent, she gave the forbidden fruit to Adam, and he willingly sinned by partaking of it with her.[55] Sensing the shame of their nakedness for the first time, Adam and Eve sewed fig leaves together to cover their nakedness with aprons.[56] The Hebrew Lexicon defines "apron" as a "loin covering, loin-cloth."[57] Loins refer to the reproductive parts around the area of the hips.

It is crucial to observe that Adam and Eve covered only their private parts, or loins. Later, God Himself visited Adam and Eve and gave them *"coats of skins."*[58] The Hebrew Lexicon defines a coat as "a long, shirt-like garment," like a tunic that covers from the breast down nearly to the feet.[59] Here we see God as the originator of modest clothing, and Adam and Eve as the originators of immodest clothing.

Adam and Eve at first chose to cover only the loins, but God chose to cover nearly the entire body, including the breasts, abdomen, and thighs. God's choice of clothing required more covering than Adam and Eve's choice, proving that God will always require more than the sinful, human mind thinks that God requires.

The ending of modest clothing, or last reference to it, is found in the Book of Revelation. White robes are the clothing that God chooses for His believers as they worship the Lamb around the throne of God in Revelation 7:9-17. The Greek Lexicon defines these white robes as "a loose outer garment...extending to the feet."[60] What a beautiful picture of God's people, worshipping Him

---

54 Genesis 2:25
55 1 Timothy 2:14
56 Genesis 3:7
57 *Voice of God Recordings Inc.*, "The Bible: Hebrew and Greek Lexicons," www.branham.org/en/messagesearch
58 Genesis 3:21
59 *Voice of God Recordings Inc.*, "The Bible: Hebrew and Greek Lexicons," www.branham.org/en/messagesearch
60 *Voice of God Recordings Inc.*, "The Bible: Hebrew and Greek Lexicons," www.branham.org/en/messagesearch

in the beauty of holiness, wearing modest, white robes that extend to their feet! You can rest assured that God's unending, eternal plan for your outward appearance is modest clothing.

TODAY IS LIKE THE DAYS OF NOAH

It has become fashionable for women to dress immodestly, or like harlots. Jesus Christ prophesied of these immoral conditions when He said that the days of His second coming would be like the days of Noah.[61] In Noah's day, the beautiful "*daughters of men*" were so attractive that the "*sons of God*" (men in the godly lineage of Adam and Seth) were intermarrying with these unbelieving women solely upon the basis of their beauty.[62] The "*daughters of men*" were unbelievers, or they would have been called the "daughters of God." These weak, compromising "*sons of God*" were just one more reason God said His Spirit would not always strive with man, and their failures helped usher in the judgment of the world-wide flood.[63] History is truly repeating itself: young men and women who are raised in godly homes are stumbling over prospective, unbelieving spouses who are immodestly dressed and marrying outside the faith of Jesus Christ. The results of these ungodly unions are generations of disobedient, faithless families.

Our spiritual eyes should see that the same evil spirits which caused the beautiful "*daughters of men*" to draw away the "*sons of God*" in the days of Noah are the same evil spirits causing men and women to stumble today because spirits do not die; they just move from one unbeliever to the next. We are living in the days of the second coming of the Son of Man, which mirror the days of Noah.

THE ROOT OF IMMODESTY

Immodesty is caused by the power of darkness, or the influence of evil spirits, that cause women and men to unclothe their bodies and present themselves immodestly before the public, as clearly written in Scripture.

61 Matthew 24:37
62 Genesis 6:2
63 Genesis 6:1-3

Two notable Bible examples demonstrate that evil spirits strip people of their clothing. First, evil spirits were credited with unclothing the man from Gadara in Luke 8:26-35. After Jesus had cast the legion of demons out of the delivered man, he was then clothed and sat at the feet of Jesus in his right mind.[64] A legion of demons stripped the poor man of his clothing, but once those demons left, he was soon fully clothed. This illustrates that someone who dresses immodestly and reveals parts of their body that God considers nakedness is not in his or her right mind.

A second example is found in Acts 19:14-16. Seven Jewish sons of Sceva were trying to cast out an evil spirit in the name of Jesus, but they were not believers in Christ or did not have genuine faith in Christ. The evil spirit from the possessed man leaped on the sons, overcame them, and prevailed against them so much so that the seven sons fled out of the house naked and wounded. The lesson is that evil spirits strip off clothing.

The power of the Holy Spirit causes us to dress modestly and keep the commandments of God. Scripture says the Holy Spirit quickens, or makes alive, the Word of God to the believer and causes him to keep God's commands.[65]

OUTWARD NAKEDNESS SIGNALS SPIRITUAL NAKEDNESS

Outward nakedness indicates spiritual nakedness. When a woman yields to the influence of evil spirits and presents her body in a sexually attractive way before the public, it is one outward sign of the inward nakedness of her soul. This means that person is not born again; she does not possess the Spirit of Jesus Christ. Her soul is naked, or absent of the Spirit's abiding presence. The Bible calls this presence the seal of the Holy Ghost.[66] A believer who is truly born again of the Holy Ghost possesses the Spirit of Christ and His righteousness, and is thereby clothed or endued with the power of God.[67] The soul of the born again Christian is clothed, or dressed, with power. The Holy Ghost has written the Word of God upon her heart.[68]

---

64 Luke 8:35
65 Ezekiel 36:27, John 6:63
66 Ephesians 1:13, 4:30
67 Luke 24:49
68 2 Corinthians 3:3

The soul's clothing is an extremely important concept. Jesus Christ's words to the church in Laodicea pronounced the most harsh denunciation to any people in human history because of their naked souls. Those in Laodicea were rich, increased of goods, had need of nothing, but were naked and did not know it.[69] The Laodiceans did not have to combat persecution, poverty, or any other life-threatening enemy. They had only to battle riches, an increase of goods, and prosperity; and yet they could not crucify the lusts of the flesh, lust of the eyes, and pride of life. Therefore, these Laodiceans deserved the greatest rebuke of all time due to their love of the world. This misplaced love proved their souls were not clothed with Christ's righteousness.

We live in the exact same state as the Laodiceans today, having increased goods, prosperity, and riches but lacking spiritual power. Thankfully, the Lord Jesus gave us the prescription on how to overcome the spirit of Laodicea—zealous repentance through communion with Christ.[70] To zealously repent means to eagerly destroy any sinful habits with an intense motivation to obey Jesus Christ. If you zealously repent, Christ will call you an overcomer and grant you a seat, or throne, near His own. After genuine repentance, your soul will be clothed with Jesus' own righteousness.

THE DANGERS OF IMMODESTY

The dangers of immodesty include causing others to stumble and being taken captive to the will of evil spirits. Any individual who dresses immodestly and leads others to lust after his or her body is guilty of sinning against Christ by leading others to stumble into sin.[71] Scripture is clear about our responsibility to present our bodies in modest apparel, for our bodies are living sacrifices unto God and temples of the Holy Ghost.[72]

Two important New Testament texts teach us a great deal about our responsibility not to set a stumbling block in anyone's way: Romans 14:12-23 and 1 Corinthians 8:7-13. In the context of these Scriptures, the examples of sins that cause others to stumble include eating meat sacrificed to idols and drinking wine. While the sin of immodest clothing is not listed in these two

---

69 Revelation 3:14-22
70 Revelation 3:19-20
71 1 Corinthians 8:12
72 Romans 12:1, 1 Corinthians 6:19, 1 Timothy 2:9

particular texts, it is listed in the following passages: Proverbs 7:10, Proverbs 6:25, and Matthew 5:28.

Proverbs 7:10 mentions the attire or clothing of a harlot. This passage brings us to the obvious conclusion that harlots or prostitutes dress in a specific, immodest way in order to tempt men to pay them for sexual sin. The harlot's clothing, or any woman's immodest clothing, ignites a man's sexual passions like a lit match ignites spilled gasoline. Additionally, consider the pure selfishness in a harlot or woman's heart to present herself immodestly, for her own gain, knowing she is weakening men's spiritual conditions and their marriages. This level of selfishness is the complete opposite of the Golden Rule, which encourages living for the benefit of others and putting their needs first: "*Therefore all things whatsoever ye would that men should do to you, do ye even so to them.*"[73]

Leading others to stumble through sinful thoughts of lust is a serious danger. Proverbs warns that men must not lust after women in their minds and that women seduce men with seductive looks.[74] Our Lord Jesus teaches that lusting in the heart is the same as committing the very act of adultery.[75] Jesus' command to avoid lusting in our hearts is part of the gospel, or good news. Those who do not hearken in repentance unto all of Christ's words, including His words about our thought-lives, will be destroyed on the day of judgment.[76] Proverbs 7:27 supports Jesus' teaching as we read about harlots leading men to hell. Whether a man stumbles at the harlot's immodest clothing, committing adultery in his heart, or fulfills the act in the flesh, he's in danger of destroying his soul.[77]

Clearly, there may be times a woman cannot keep a lustful man from having evil thoughts about her even though she has dressed modestly. In this case, the woman is innocent if she followed God's command for modest clothing. The person lusting is the only guilty one. Many men are so addicted to lust that they will fulfill their evil thoughts about a modestly dressed woman despite her efforts to honor God. In our hypersexualized culture, women are now becoming as lustful as men, so it increasingly important for both sexes to avoid inciting sexual passions by dressing modestly. Titus 1:15 states that the pure in heart are not guilty of someone else's sin, saying: "*Unto the pure all*

---

73 Matthew 7:12
74 Proverbs 6:25
75 Matthew 5:28
76 Acts 3:22-23
77 Proverbs 6:32

things are pure: but unto them that are defiled and unbelieving is nothing pure; but even their mind and conscience is defiled." God's principle from Genesis 18:23 declares that He will not destroy the righteous with the wicked, so can you rest assured that God will not hold you responsible for another person's lust if you are dressed modestly.

Being taken captive by an evil spirit, or trapped in addiction, is another danger of immodest clothing. Addiction can take place only when a person willingly submits to the evil spirit by his or her own free will, since the devil cannot make us do evil.[78] An addict is in a slave-like condition where he or she is under such a strong demonic influence that he or she regularly obeys an evil spirit and does not have the power or faith to obey Christ's Word. Jesus described this condition as being bound by a greater power and being spoiled from all godly possessions, including joy, faith, hope, love, and other godly blessings.[79] Being trapped in an addiction is commonly called captivity in Scripture.[80]

Lust addicts live completely contrary to God's calling to be His children.[81] Obeying fleshly, sexual lusts makes men and women resemble beasts[82] rather than children of God. Beastly, lustful behavior is responsible for many evils in society, such as divorces, pornography, sexual violence, and sexually transmitted diseases. A sensual, carnal lifestyle is proof that the Holy Spirit is absent from a person's life.[83]

The only hope for an addicted individual is repentance, which starts with confessing his sin and exposing the evil spirit in his life. Once the sin is confessed and forgiven by the blood of Jesus Christ, Satan's evil spirit no longer has the power or influence it once had. The individual can now resist the devil or evil spirit with a righteous vengeance.[84] If a believer continually resists the temptation and stands faithful in obedience to God's Word, the evil spirit must flee from him according to the promise of God.[85]

---

78 James 1:14
79 Matthew 12:28-29
80 Matthew 12:28-29, 43-45, 1 Corinthians 6:12, 2 Timothy 2:26
81 Matthew 5:9
82 Jude 1:10
83 James 3:15, Jude 1:19
84 2 Corinthians 7:10-11
85 James 4:7

MY EXPERIENCE WITH IMMODESTY

Modest clothing, holiness in appearance, and God-honoring hair length were certainly not a big part of my background. While I have many reasons to be thankful for being raised in a home that attended a charismatic, denominational church, my siblings and I learned very little about modesty and holiness perhaps because my parents were not taught God's standards in these areas.

In fall of 2001, as a 21 year old college student, I first learned about God's standards for a holy appearance. I quickly changed churches so I could hear more truth preached every service. Upon hearing and reading the Bible truth about these subjects, the Bible felt like a new book to me. By worshipping with new believers in a church that believed in God's modesty and holiness standards, I quickly gained the understanding that God wanted all believers to walk according to the *"same rule"* or standard of investigating, judging, living and acting.[86] As I witnessed first hand a group of Spirit-led believers who wore modest clothes and kept holiness standards, I immediately felt the presence of the Holy Ghost in a greater way than I had ever felt before.

Seeing other believers obey this higher level of modesty and holiness made me hunger to duplicate this same degree of dedication in my own life, which Jesus called a hunger and thirst for righteousness.[87] After months of persistent prayer and study, the Lord led me to make two major changes. First, I began to dress modestly at all times. I stopped taking off my shirt to pridefully show off my upper body. In the past, I had enjoyed undressing in order to get compliments and even heard females do the "wolf whistle" at me. Second, the Holy Spirit led me to cut my hair—which at the time resembled the mullet look—as I wanted to honor the Lord with my hair by making it look undoubtedly masculine.

I'd like to share a personal story from my childhood about the devastating effects that immodesty had upon my young mind which led to years of addiction to the spirit of lust. As a child in Sunday School, I remember singing, "Be careful little eyes what you see" but it seems I was almost powerless to overcome the temptation of immodestly dressed women when first presented with the temptation. For certain, I was unaware that the Bible taught temptation would

---

86 Philippians 3:16
87 Matthew 5:6

always come in three channels—lust of the eyes, lust of the flesh, and the pride of life.[88]

My story begins when I was in grade school and one of my friends invited me to spend the night at his house. While there, we traded baseball cards, but late into the night, we started watching MTV with his older brother. My eyes were glued to the screen as I witnessed music, clothing, and dancing I had never seen before. Those few moments had a lasting effect upon my mind. When I returned home the next day, those images of immodestly dressed women remained in my mind, along with the explicitly sexual lyrics.

After a short time passed, our family was sitting down to enjoy our weekly ritual of watching the Cosby Show. Normally, I was front and center of the television, sure not to miss one second of the show I thought was the funniest of all.

But this night was different. Because of the immodest clothing and dancing I had witnessed at my friend's house, I was off in my bedroom all alone drawing women in bikinis on baseball cards. The music, dancing, and immodest clothing of MTV had so captured my mind that I combined the new, lustful images in my mind—sexy clothing—with my childhood hobby, baseball card trading. My mind was officially addicted to the spirit of lust.

At some point during the Cosby Show, my mother walked into the room and asked me what I was doing. Instantly I felt ashamed and embarrassed and my mother confiscated my homemade "baseball cards." My mother was not one to purposely embarrass me, but she would try to separate me from evil. I have never forgotten this moment and now that I have a greater understanding of the Bible and spiritual matters, I can easily see how the spirit of lust entered and filled my mind through seeing immodestly dressed women on MTV.

As the years passed, I would jump upon every opportunity to watch TV shows, commercials, or movies with immodestly dressed women. The lustful images filled my mind and I let the stronger spirit of lust spoil the spiritual blessings from my mind and heart.

When I was in my late teens, another friend introduced me to free pornographic material on the internet and I spent the next few years under a greater bondage to the lust of the eyes. This addiction continued into my college

---

88 1 John 2:16

years and I remember renting the library's laptops to write papers but spent substantial time on lustful websites.

By the grace of Almighty God through much prayer, Bible study, and hearing the preaching of the Word of God, I was given complete victory over the pornographic empire around 2002 and have never gone back. The goodness of God brought me to true repentance and I confessed my sin and shame to my Heavenly Father. I remain ever grateful to God that He delivered me from this evil spirit of lust before I entered into my marriage covenant with my darling wife.

These memories of my childhood have created a strong desire in my heart and soul to protect myself and my children from the evil spirits that promote immodest clothing, and ultimately, a sin-slaved, ungodly life. While I am ashamed that I became addicted to the spirit of lust at 8 years old, I am eternally thankful that God has delivered me from this evil spirit and has given me the Scriptures I needed to personally overcome this spirit and help others do the same.

CONCLUSION

The Word of God is the one and only foundation we need for our lives. God wants us to live in a way that fulfills the holy purpose spelled out in Scripture.

Modesty matters to God's people because it is commanded. Christians recognize the short and long term effects of immodesty and choose to cast down any and all of Satan's lustful temptations that contradict the Word of God. Although Satan constantly exalts immodesty through the addictive spirit of lust, God's promises provide every single spiritual blessing we need for our journey. Christians obtain these blessings by Christ's own gift of faith.[89] Using His faith, we obey God's holy calling for a God-honoring outward appearance. Our consciences rest assured that God sees our lives as obedient and beautiful.

With the understanding that the eternal Word of God is our sure foundation, we can now learn how to apply Scripture to our lives.

---

89   Galatians 2:20, Ephesians 1:3

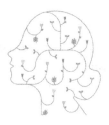

CHAPTER 2

How To Apply Old Testament Scripture To The New Testament

"And there shall in no wise enter into it any thing that defileth, neither whatsoever worketh abomination, or maketh a lie: but they which are written in the Lamb's book of life."

—Revelation 21:27

New Testament believers need the Old Testament for a variety of reasons. Peter instructed believers to live holy lives and be mindful of Old Testament Scripture because its fulfillment was guaranteed.[90] Paul wrote that we must learn from it and admonished us to remember the decisions of rebellious Israel on their journey from Egypt to Canaan that we might take heed lest we fall into similar temptations.[91] All Scripture, which includes Old Testament writings, is profitable for doctrine, reproof, correction, and instruction in righteousness.[92]

RIGHTLY DIVIDING THE OLD TESTAMENT SCRIPTURE

New Testament teachers must rightly divide the Word of truth.[93] Old Testament Scripture is to be rightly divided, or placed in one or more of the nine following categories:

90 2 Peter 3:1-12
91 Romans 15:1-4, 1 Corinthians 10:1-14
92 2 Timothy 3:16-17
93 2 Timothy 2:15

- Ceremonial laws not in effect for Christians (but in effect for Jews)
- Laws not in effect for Christians (but in effect for Jews)
- Moral laws still in effect for Jews and Christians
- Allegorical truths for Christians
- Foreshadowing for Christians
- Direct prophecy for Jews and Christians
- History for Jews and Christians
- Wisdom for Jews and Christians
- Psalms for Jews and Christians

These nine categories provide structure for correctly placing Scripture, but are not meant to limit a passage to only one category. Passages can be placed in multiple categories. For example, Genesis 22:8 says, *"And Abraham said, my son, God will provide Himself a lamb for a burnt offering: so they went both of them together."* As a New Testament teacher, I can place this Scripture in three of the nine categories: foreshadowing for Christians, direct prophecy for Jews and Christians, and history for Jews and Christians. Genesis 22:8 is foreshadowing for Christians because God provided a lamb for Abraham that foreshadowed Him providing Jesus Christ, the *"Lamb of God,"* for Abraham's seed.[94] Direct prophecy for Jews and Christians is a fitting category because God was prophesying that He alone would prepare the body of Jesus Christ to be a sacrifice for the sins of the whole world—Jews and Gentiles included—just as He alone prepared the lamb to take Isaac's place on Mt. Moriah.[95] Genesis 22:8 is history for Jews and Christians because both groups can agree that the details and events of the passage are factual.

I must clarify the difference between Christians and Jews. Christians recognize Jesus Christ as the promised Messiah, the Christ, the Redeemer of mankind, and the One who fulfilled all the Old Testament prophecy about the Son of God. Furthermore, Christians are those who have repented of their sins, been baptized in the name of the Lord Jesus, been born again of the Spirit of God, and are observing all of Jesus' commands. Jews, on the other hand, do not believe Jesus Christ fulfilled the prophecies about their promised Messiah. True Jews obey the law of Moses and have a zeal for God but do not have the

---

94 John 1:29, Galatians 3:29
95 Ephesians 2:11-22, Hebrews 10:5

knowledge that Jesus Christ is their Messiah.[96] When Israel rejected Jesus as their Messiah, God chose to blind the eyes of the Jews from believing in Jesus Christ in order that He might save the Gentiles.[97]

THE NINE CATEGORIES

First, ceremonial laws are Old Testament laws that pertained to the Aaronic priesthood that are no longer in effect for New Testament believers, but are in effect for Jews. Some examples of these laws include sacrificing animals, physical requirements for ministers, and hereditary requirements for the priesthood.[98] However, Orthodox Jews do not carry out the ceremonial laws because they lack a temple.

Second, Old Testament laws that are no longer in effect in the New Testament include various laws such as circumcision,[99] prohibited foods,[100] and the instant death penalty for blasphemy.[101] These laws were given to Israel through the prophet Moses to all the children of Israel but are no longer in effect in the New Testament.

Third, there are many moral laws from the Old Testament that are still in effect today, including the 10 Commandments, numerous abominations, and tithing. The 10 Commandments of Moses are still in effect in the New Testament, as shown in Figure 1, although Saturday Sabbath-keeping has a different application for Christians. A separate section of this chapter addresses the fourth commandment. The abominations of homosexuality, justifying the wicked, worshipping graven images and partaking in idolatry are still abominable in the sight of God today for New Testament believers.

---

96 Romans 10:2
97 Romans 11:7-11
98 Hebrews 7:11-28
99 Exodus 12:48, Leviticus 12:3, Galatians 6:15
100 Leviticus 11:4-6, Acts 10:9-16, 1 Timothy 4:4-5
101 Leviticus 24:14, Acts 13:45-46, 1 Timothy 1:13

Figure 1

Ten Commandments Exodus 20:1-17	New Testament Scripture
I. No other gods before Me STILL IN EFFECT	Matthew 4:10 *Then saith Jesus unto him, Get thee hence, Satan: for it is written, Thou shalt worship the Lord thy God, and him only shalt thou serve.*
2. Make no graven images STILL IN EFFECT	Revelation 9:20 *And the rest of the men which were not killed by these plagues yet repented not of the works of their hands, that they should not worship devils, and idols of gold, and silver, and brass, and stone, and wood: which neither can see, nor hear, nor walk:* Acts 17:29 *Forasmuch then as we are the offspring of God, we ought not to think that the Godhead is like unto gold, or silver, or stone, graven by art and man's device. And the times of this ignorance God winked at; but now commandeth all men every where to repent:*
III. Do not take the name of the Lord in vain STILL IN EFFECT	Matthew 6:9 *After this manner therefore pray ye: Our Father which art in heaven, Hallowed be thy name.*

IV. Keep Sabbath day holy NEW APPLICATION The New Testament Sabbath is the believer resting or ceasing from his sinful works and then doing the works of the Holy Ghost. This spiritual rest begins when a person is born again of the Holy Ghost (Isaiah 28:11-12, 1 Corinthians 14:21-22, Hebrews 4:1-12).	Hebrews 4:9 *There remaineth therefore a rest to the people of God. For he that is entered into his rest, he also hath ceased from his own works, as God [did] from his. Let us labour therefore to enter into that rest, lest any man fall after the same example of unbelief.* Matthew 11:28 *Come unto me, all [ye] that labour and are heavy laden, and I will give you rest. Take my yoke upon you, and learn of me; for I am meek and lowly in heart: and ye shall find rest unto your souls.*
V. Honor thy mother and father STILL IN EFFECT	Ephesians 6:1-3 *Children, obey your parents in the Lord: for this is right. Honour thy father and mother; (which is the first commandment with promise;) That it may be well with thee, and thou mayest live long on the earth.*
VI. Thou shalt not kill STILL IN EFFECT	Galatians 5:21 *Envyings, murders, drunkenness, revellings, and such like: of the which I tell you before, as I have also told you in time past, that they which do such things shall not inherit the kingdom of God.*

VII. Thou shalt not commit adultery STILL IN EFFECT	**1 Corinthians 6:9-10** *Know ye not that the unrighteous shall not inherit the kingdom of God? Be not deceived: neither fornicators, nor idolaters, nor adulterers, nor effeminate, nor abusers of themselves with mankind, Nor thieves, nor covetous, nor drunkards, nor revilers, nor extortioners, shall inherit the kingdom of God.*
VIII. Thou shalt not steal STILL IN EFFECT	**1 Corinthians 6:10** *Nor thieves, nor covetous, nor drunkards, nor revilers, nor extortioners, shall inherit the kingdom of God.*
IX Thou shalt not bear false witness STILL IN EFFECT	**Ephesians 4:25** *Wherefore putting away lying, speak every man truth with his neighbour: for we are members one of another.*
X. Thou shalt not covet STILL IN EFFECT	**1 Corinthians 6:10** *Nor thieves, nor covetous, nor drunkards, nor revilers, nor extortioners, shall inherit the kingdom of God.*

Fourth, there is a category called allegorical truths that certain Old Testament Scriptures can be placed into for our learning. Allegories are symbolic expressions that are interpreted to reveal a hidden meaning. Examples include Ishmael and Isaac, Manasseh and Ephraim, and Abraham's faith in Isaac as his seed. Ishmael, the son of the bondwoman Hagar, represents those under the Old Testament law who were trying to earn salvation through their own fleshly efforts. Isaac represented New Testament believers who were believing the promises of God by faith and were saved by grace.[102] Manasseh, the first-born son, represents the Jews, who should have received Christ as their Messiah, as He was first sent to them.[103] Ephraim, the younger, represents the Gentiles, who received the blessing through the cross, or crossed hands of their grandfather, Jacob.[104] Galatians declares the blessing of Abraham came upon the Gentiles through the cross of Jesus Christ.[105] Although God asked Abraham to sacrifice his son, Isaac, Hebrews teaches that Abraham had accounted that God was able to raise him up from the dead.[106] Instead, God provided a ram to die in Isaac's place and Abraham *"received him in a figure,"* or allegory of Jesus Christ taking our place in death.[107]

Foreshadowing for Christians is the fifth category and are referred to as types. Types foretell someone or some event to come in the future. Examples of types include the role of Joseph as savior and Abraham's divinely-provided ram as a substitutionary sacrifice. Joseph, son of Jacob, was a type of Jesus Christ, as he was sold for 20 pieces of silver which foreshadowed Jesus being sold for 30 pieces of silver.[108] This fifth category requires Bible teachers to be careful how they interpret types, as not all types are a perfect match, like the example of Joseph being sold for 20 pieces of silver and yet Jesus was sold for 30 pieces. Just as Joseph was falsely accused and put in prison, so was Jesus arrested falsely.[109] While incarcerated, Joseph and Jesus were both surrounded by two men—one lived and one died.[110] Abraham's divinely-provided ram as a sacrifice foreshadowed Jesus as God's provided sacrifice for mankind. The ram took

---

102 Galatians 4:21-24
103 Matthew 10:5-6
104 Genesis 48:1-19
105 Galatians 3:13-14
106 Hebrews 11:18-19
107 Genesis 22:13, Romans 5:8
108 Genesis 37:28, Matthew 26:15
109 Genesis 39:1-23, Luke 23:14, 15, 41
110 Genesis 40:1-23, Luke 23:39-43

the place of Abraham's son, or seed. Likewise, God supernaturally prepared the body of Jesus Christ, through the Spirit's conception in the womb of the virgin Mary, and led His Son to die for Abraham's spiritual seed.[111]

There is an exciting, prophetic aspect to foreshadowing. At times the Holy Spirit speaks through Old Testament stories to instruct us regarding future events, such as the second coming of Jesus Christ. We can use the life of Joseph, son of Jacob, for an example of the second coming of Christ. Joseph and his brothers represent Jesus and His brethren, the Jewish people. We know Joseph's brothers were "blinded" to his identity when they went to Egypt to request food but Joseph eventually revealed his identity to them and saved their lives. Scripture teaches that Joseph put out everyone from before him, which would have included his wife, when he revealed his identity to his brothers. Allegorically, we know the Scriptural fact that Jesus' brethren, the Jews, are currently blinded to His identity as their Messiah so that the Gentiles can be saved.[112] But one day Jesus will reveal His true identity to the Jews and He will save them from their sins. Christ will seal them with the baptism of the Holy Ghost, which is the "*seal*" of God, described as the seal of God "*in their foreheads.*"[113] This foreshadow helps teach that the "wife" of Jesus Christ, the New Testament Gentile believers, will be gone from the earth and raptured up into heaven while Jesus stands on Mount Zion and reveals His identity to His brethren, the 144,000 believing Israelis.[114]

The sixth category is direct prophecy, and three examples of this category are the rapture, the new heavens and earth, and Jesus' resurrection. Regarding the rapture, it is striking to find that Paul used Isaiah 25:8 as a direct prophecy for the Gentile church in 1 Corinthians 15:54. We should learn a critical lesson in this category: the Holy Ghost can seemingly pull out a Scripture from any Old Testament location and apply it to the New Testament believer in any way He purposes. God's ways are past finding out. He is the author of the Word and thereby is the only One that knows how to correctly interpret Scripture. The new heavens and new earth are direct prophecies found in both the Old and New Testaments.[115] Peter echoes Isaiah's prophecy and then reminds us to be diligent and steadfast in our walk with the Lord. Jesus' resurrection is

---

111 Romans 4:16, Galatians 3:16, 29, Hebrews 10:5
112 Romans 11:7
113 Revelation 7:3, 9:4
114 Revelation 14:1
115 Isaiah 65:17, 2 Peter 3:13

directly prophesied by David in Psalm 16:10 and then recorded as fulfilled in Acts 2:27.

History, wisdom, and psalms are the final three categories. Old Testament history includes all the events and details from the creation of the world in Genesis until the conclusion of the Book of Malachi. Books of wisdom include Proverbs and Ecclesiastes. The psalms include 150 songs that focus on the themes of God's glory and wisdom. Numerous songs are prayers to God and also include heartfelt lamentations that both Jews and Gentiles can appreciate.

THE NEW TESTAMENT SABBATH

The Saturday Sabbath day is the only command of the 10 Commandments that has a new application for Christians. Christians must not be deceived into thinking they will be lost if they work on Saturday. Although there are physical and spiritual benefits to slowing down our lifestyles, Jesus taught that there is something greater than just resting one day of the week.

Jesus Christ offered rest for our souls, not just rest for our bodies![116] After His resurrection, Christ breathed on His disciples, constraining them to receive the born-again experience, the baptism of the Holy Ghost.[117] The obedient disciples honored their Master and did indeed receive the born-again experience, or soul-rest, as recorded in Acts chapter 2. Soul-rest means that Jesus wants us to rest completely from our sinful works.[118] The New Testament Sabbath is for the Christian to be born again of the Holy Spirit, and to trust or rest in God.

The prophet Isaiah foretold this born-again experience, or soul-rest, more than 700 years before Jesus Christ lived on the earth. Isaiah said, *"For with stammering lips and another tongue will he speak to this people. To whom he said, This is the rest wherewith ye may cause the weary to rest; and this is the refreshing: yet they would not hear."*[119] Notice that Isaiah plainly said, *"This is the rest!"* The new rest is connected to God using stammering lips to speak to His people, which is fulfilled in Acts chapter 2, for they spoke with tongues as the Spirit gave them utterance.[120] In 1 Corinthians 14:21, Paul later quotes Isaiah 28:11-

---

116 Matthew 11:29
117 John 20:22, Acts 1:5
118 Hebrews 4:10
119 Isaiah 28:11-12
120 Acts 2:4

12 and connects it to the tongues that were given to the Jews and all other unbelieving nations in Acts chapter 2.

Paul wrote that Saturday Sabbath days were a *"shadow of things to come"* in Colossians 2:16-17. God's purpose of Saturday Sabbath-keeping in the Old Testament points to something greater to come. Jesus teaches that the true rest is the born-again experience He proclaims in John 3:7 and 7:37-39. In reference to believers receiving the Holy Ghost, Jesus says, *"Ye must be born again"* and *"If any man thirst, let him come unto me, and drink. He that believeth on me, as the scripture hath said, out of his belly shall flow rivers of living water."*

In the born-again experience, a Christian rests or walks according to the Spirit and does not fulfill the lusts of the flesh.[121] For the remainder of his earthly walk, the Spirit-filled Christian will rest, or cease, from doing lustful, sinful habits and will do works that please God. Now that's a true rest! I would much rather rest from my sinful works every day of my life than just relaxing on each Saturday but continue in sinful works.

If you can see the truth about the spiritual rest God is offering today and enter into that rest, your obedience will delight the Lord Jesus Christ! Our God delights more in constant, daily rest from sin than just physically resting one day of the week. Thankfully, if we truly receive the baptism of the Holy Ghost and rest from our sinful lives, we will actually have a physical day of rest built into our week, which is Sunday. How great is the wisdom of our God! Just as the early Christians met on the first day of the week,[122] so we meet every Sunday to honor the resurrection of Jesus Christ. True Christians will not forsake the assembling of the saints on the first day of the week because sincere meetings provide spiritual meat, edification, comfort, consolation, and more.[123]

TWO OR THREE WITNESSES

The Holy Spirit guides Bible teachers to correctly categorize an Old Testament Scripture in one or more of the nine categories. To prove the classification is correct, the Spirit provides the teachers with *"two or three witnesses"* from other Bible passages. Jesus and Paul both speak of the necessity of having multiple

---

121 Galatians 5:24-25
122 Acts 20:7
123 Hebrews 10:25

witnesses to establish a word of truth.[124] Isaiah writes a similar thought that doctrine, or instruction, must be built line upon line, precept upon precept.[125] Faithful Bible teachers use more than one Scripture to support their beliefs.

Three doctrinal examples of using two or three Scriptural witnesses to prove that an Old Testament command remains binding in the New Testament are the sin of homosexuality, the command for children to honor their parents, and paying tithes to one's local church. All three of these subjects are relevant to and essential for today's world.

The sin of homosexuality was an abomination in the Old Testament and is still a sin today. Homosexuality has multiple Old Testament witnesses to establish it as a sin.[126] Three New Testament witnesses establish this act as a deplorable sin: Romans 1:26-32, 1 Corinthians 6:9-11, and 1 Timothy 1:10-11. With *"two or three witnesses"* in both the Old and New Testaments, homosexuality is easily placed in the category of moral laws still in effect for Jews and Christians.

The fifth commandment of Moses, for children to honor their parents, is taught in the Old Testament in Exodus 20:12 and Deuteronomy 5:16. But is this command still required today? Yes, because the fifth command has two New Testament Bible witnesses: Matthew 19:19 and Ephesians 6:1-2. Just as in the case of homosexuality, we conclude from the multiple Bible witnesses that children must honor their parents as a binding command in the New Testament. Faithful Bible teachers place this command in the category of moral laws still in effect for Jews and Christians.

A third example is tithing ten percent of your income to your local church. In the Old Testament, tithing predated the law of Moses, as both Abraham and Jacob tithed.[127] Leviticus 27:30 and Deuteronomy 12:11 are two of the numerous Scriptures that commanded tithing in the Old Testament. But is tithing a New Testament command? Yes, there are five reasons tithing is still a New Testament command and should be placed in the category of moral laws still in effect for Jews and Christians. First, the New Testament never abolishes tithing. Second, Jesus said tithing was one of the least of the commands, which means it is still a command.[128] Third, Jesus never stopped anyone from paying

---

124 Matthew 18:16, 2 Corinthians 13:1
125 Isaiah 28:9-10
126 Leviticus 18:22, 20:13
127 Genesis 14:20, 28:22
128 Matthew 23:23

tithes. Fourth, Paul teaches that the ministers who preach the gospel should live of the gospel in 1 Corinthians 9:9 and 14. The apostle referenced the Old Testament lesson of not muzzling the ox that treads out of the corn and applied it to New Testament preachers.[129] Last, Hebrews records that Abraham willingly paid tithes to Melchisedec, Who was God in a flesh body, as a prefigure of the true High Priest, Jesus Christ.[130] Since Abraham, the father of faith, paid tithes without a written command, the Holy Spirit compels Christians to pay tithes and offerings because believers are the children, or seed of Abraham, through faith in Jesus Christ.[131]

WE ARE NOT UNDER THE LAW

One common phrase I often hear in reply to my Bible teaching on doctrine is "We are not under the Old Testament." However, Paul often uses Old Testament Scripture to provide authority for New Testament living. There is value in teaching from the entire Bible, as Paul said, *"All Scripture is given by inspiration of God, and is profitable for doctrine, for reproof, for correction, for instruction in righteousness."*[132]

Clearly, we are not obligated to fulfill every commandment in the Old Testament. All the ceremonial laws of sacrificial rituals were a *"shadow of good things to come"* that Jesus Christ's crucifixion fulfilled.[133] Christ declared, *"It is finished"* on the cross, signaling the end to the Aaronic priesthood and beginning of the new covenant with better promises.[134]

Paul's writings from Romans and Galatians teach that we are *"not under the law,"* meaning we are not saved by our individual works or by our own righteousness.[135] The law has the power to curse anyone who does not keep every single Old Testament commandment. In contrast, New Testament believers are saved by grace through faith in Jesus Christ, for Christ bore the curse of God for our sins on the cross of Calvary.[136]

---

129 Deuteronomy 25:4
130 Hebrews 7:2, 4
131 Galatians 3:29
132 2 Timothy 3:16
133 Hebrews 10:1-18
134 Hebrews 7:12, 8:6
135 Romans 4:1-16, 6:14-15, Galatians 2:21, 3:23, 5:4
136 Galatians 3:9-14, Ephesians 2:8-10

Thus, the phrase, "We are not under the Old Testament" is true but must be applied correctly. New Testament teachers should use appropriate Old Testament Scripture to build doctrine, as Paul did in Ephesians and 1 Corinthians. Paul affirmed the 5th Commandment that children should honor their parents.[137] If Christians are "not under the Old Testament," then where did Paul get his authority to teach that children are to obey their parents and also promise them a long life on the earth? Paul's authority to teach the 5th commandment to Christians came from Jesus, as he was taught his gospel "*by the revelation of Jesus Christ.*"[138] It's clear that the 5th commandment is categorized as a moral law still in effect for Jews and Christians. The righteousness of the law is still important to God today. When Christians walk in obedience to the Holy Spirit, they are fulfilling the righteousness of the law.[139]

1 Corinthians 15:51-58 also demonstrates Paul's reliance on the Old Testament passages as foundation for New Testament truths. While writing about the future event of the rapture, the Holy Spirit inspired Paul to use the same Bible phrase as the prophet Isaiah, "*Death is swallowed up in victory,*" written over 800 years earlier.[140] Thus, both Isaiah and Paul were preparing us for the catching away of the Spirit-filled saints, as we look "*for that blessed hope, and the glorious appearing of the great God and our Savior, Jesus Christ.*"[141] Isaiah 25:8 is categorized as direct prophecy for Jews and Christians

Along with these two examples, the New Testament is replete with references to God's Words from the Old Covenant. Bible teachers must use the Old Testament as directed by the Holy Ghost. We owe it to ourselves and those in our realm of influence to continue to study and understand the Old Testament as the Spirit of truth guides us to rightly divide the Word of truth.

A study into New Testament teaching will help you understand that we are to fulfill the "*righteousness of the law*" according to Romans 8:4. Christians should willingly choose to obey God's Word, obeying the will of the Holy Spirit. The law that we are currently under is the "*law of the Spirit.*"[142] This holy law will never lead us into sin, but rather into complete obedience to the Word of God. Jesus walked in the "*law of the Spirit*" in His life because the Spirit

---

137 Ephesians 6:1-3
138 Galatians 1:11-12
139 Romans 8:4
140 Isaiah 25:8
141 Titus 2:13
142 Romans 8:2

abode upon Him.[143] The Spirit led Christ into full obedience to the Word of God and so the Spirit will lead our lives the exact same way.

The law of Moses was holy, just, and good, but without the power of the New Testament relationship with God, the believer could not fulfill the righteousness of the law. Christians today should not despise the law of Moses, but rather desire to obey the holy nature of the law and those righteous commands that God has carried over into the New Testament. Obeying the holy nature is possible because God's Spirit now writes His law upon the fleshy tables of our hearts.[144] God's nature has become our nature.

BLANKET STATEMENTS

"We are not under the law" seems to be a blanket statement that people use who do not want to hear Old Testament Scripture used to teach New Testament believers. Believers are called to grow in the knowledge and understanding of God.[145] Christians should never answer a matter before hearing it, as modeled by the saints in Berea, who searched the Scripture daily to determine the truth of Paul's preaching.[146] Proverbs says answering a matter too soon, without studying it out is a shame and sign of folly.[147]

Some blanket statements are true, or partially true, while others are false. I want to give examples of each kind of statement to help the reader learn how to rightly divide every blanket statement, for every blanket statement needs "*two or three witnesses*" to prove it true.

A well known blanket statement that is true is "Jesus Christ is the only way to the Father and no one gets to heaven except through Christ." This is true based upon John 14:6, Acts 4:12, and Matthew 25:31-46. Most Bible readers are very familiar with John 14:6 and Acts 4:12, but Matthew 25:31-46 provides additional support to the fact that no one will enter eternal life except through the mercy of Jesus Christ. In this scene of separation on the Day of Judgment, we see Jesus granting eternal life to surprised individuals. These surprised ones question, "When did we help You, thereby deserving eternal

---

143 John 1:32
144 2 Corinthians 3:3
145 2 Peter 3:18
146 Acts 17:11
147 Proverbs 18:13

life?" This question shows two great truths. First, the least Christian is a genuine representation and ambassador of Jesus Christ on this earth, although not recognized as such by the world. Some who do good acts to the least known Christians will receive eternal life from Jesus Christ. Second, there will be surprises on the Day of Judgment. From this text, it seems possible that perhaps Muslims, Buddhists, or members of other faiths that reject Jesus Christ as Savior may be granted eternal life simply due to their treatment of His faithful followers, the true Christians. Perhaps Gamaliel and Nicodemus will be granted life because they stood for Christians in times of trouble.

Here are some true blanket statements regarding Bible doctrine that may surprise you but yet are 100% accurate with at least *"two or three witnesses"* from Scripture:

- No person in the New Testament was ever recorded as being baptized in the titles, "Father, Son, and Holy Ghost." All recorded baptisms used the literal name of "Jesus Christ," "Lord Jesus," or "Lord."[148]

- God never asked one godly woman to cut or trim her hair. Instead, all godly women had uncut hair as seen in numerous texts: John 12:1-8, Luke 7:36-50, 1 Corinthians 11:1-16, and Revelation 9:8.

- God never called Himself "three persons" because He is one person.[149] Instead, He said He was the only God and there was no one beside Him.[150]

- Jesus was never called the "second person" because He is the physical image of God's one person.[151] Instead, He was called Emmanuel, Mighty God, and Everlasting Father.[152]

- Jesus never called a woman to be an apostle. Our Lord called only men to be apostles.[153] Additionally, Paul forbade any woman from teaching men: 1 Timothy 2:12, 1 Corinthians 14:34-35.

---

148 Acts 2:38, 8:16, 10:48, 19:5, 22:16
149 Job 13:8
150 Isaiah 43:11, 44:6, 8
151 Colossians 1:15, Hebrews 1:3
152 Matthew 1:23, Isaiah 9:6
153 Matthew 10:1-4

- The apostles never asked anyone if they wanted to "invite" Jesus into their hearts for salvation. Instead, the apostles preached repentance, immersion in water, and the infilling of the Holy Ghost.[154]

This list could indeed grow, but I hope it opens your eyes to the fact that much of modern Christendom has strayed from teaching sound, Bible doctrine. Before making a blanket statement about the Bible, search the Scriptures to answer each question that may come to your mind.

ABOMINATIONS

An abomination is one specific type of moral law that means a "disgusting thing" in the sight of God, according to the Hebrew Lexicon.[155] Deuteronomy 12:31 states that God hates abominations. God's holy, eternal city, the New Jerusalem, will not have any abominable work within its domain.[156] Since there are 166 Scriptures that mention abominations, it behooves us to know which acts are abominations in the sight of God today because we want to live in the New Jerusalem with Christ Jesus for all eternity.

After reading all 166 abomination Scriptures, I have found three Old Testament abominations that are no longer abominable in the sight of God for the New Testament believer: eating a peace offering on the third day,[157] offering a blemished animal sacrifice,[158] and eating unclean foods.[159]

Eating a peace offering on the third day is no longer an abomination because New Testament believers are no longer required to offer animal sacrifices, as Jesus Christ was the *"once for all"* sacrifice that God has provided for believers.[160] Jesus is both our offering and peace,[161] as we have peace with God through our Lord Jesus Christ.[162]

Offering a blemished animal sacrifice is no longer an abomination in the

---

154 Acts 2:37-39, 3;19, 8:21-23, 9:17, 17:30, 19:1-7, 26:20
155 *Voice of God Recordings Inc.*, "The Bible: Hebrew and Greek Lexicons," www.branham.org/en/messagesearch
156 Revelation 21:27
157 Leviticus 7:18
158 Deuteronomy 17:1
159 Leviticus 9:11-43
160 Hebrews 10:1-10
161 Ephesians 2:14, 5:2
162 Romans 5:1

New Testament because we have already established that God gave us the offering of the body of Jesus Christ to replace the blood of bulls and goats.[163] But it is important to note that our worship in the New Testament must be according to the Spirit and truth, or else the worship is offered in vain.[164] There is a spiritual application of this Old Testament abomination that we can apply to our worship today, as we must offer our bodies as a living sacrifice unto God.[165]

Unclean foods from the Israeli diet are no longer abominations for the New Testament believer, as evidenced through Peter's heavenly vision in Acts 10:9-18. The fact that God did away with these dietary abominations was so surprising that Peter told the Lord "*Not so*" three times after the Lord instructed him to "*rise, kill, and eat*" all manner of four-footed beasts, wild beasts, creeping things, and fowls of the air. Paul's teaching supports God's visions to Peter, saying, "*For every creature of God is good, and nothing to be refused, if it be received with thanksgiving: For it is sanctified by the word of God and prayer.*"[166] The only dietary restrictions for Christians are not eating blood, strangled animals, or foods dedicated unto idols.[167]

Here is a partial list of the abominations that still remain detestable to God and the New Testament believer, and are categorized as moral laws still in effect for Jews and Christians. Note that each abomination has at least "*two or three witnesses*" according to the rule for establishing an Old Testament moral law as a binding command for the New Testament believer.

- Justifying sin (Proverbs 17:15, 2 Thessalonians 2:10-12, Jude 4)
- Homosexuality (1 Corinthians 6:9, Romans 1:26-32, 1 Timothy 1:10)
- Idolatry and graven images (Galatians 5:20-21, Revelation 13:14-15, 21:8, 22:14-15)
- Murder (Deuteronomy 12:31, Revelation 21:8)
- Witchcraft (Deuteronomy 18:11-12, Galatians 5:20-21)
- Worshipping with a wicked heart (Proverbs 15:8, Matthew 7:21-23)
- Diverse weights and measures, or extortion (Deuteronomy 25:13-16, 1 Corinthians 6:10)

---

163 Hebrews 10:1-10
164 Matthew 15:9, John 4:23-24
165 Romans 12:1-2
166 1 Timothy 4:4-5
167 Acts 15:20, 1 Corinthians 8:7, Revelation 2:14

- Froward, perverse, or wicked thoughts, hearts, and ways (Proverbs 3:32, 15:9, 26; Acts 20:29-30)
- Seven abominations of Proverbs 6:16-19: pride, lying, murder, wicked thoughts, pursuing mischief, false witness, sowing discord (1 John 2:16, Revelation 21:8, Romans 1:29-32, Acts 13:10, Romans 13:9, Romans 16:17-18)

God's immutable character allows us to rightly divide the actions that either gain His approval or disapproval, blessing or curse. As Satan increases his attacks against the true church, faithful Bible teachers need to continue giving more of their time, focus, attention, and energy into denouncing abominations and feeding the people of God the truth. True doctrine will save both the preacher and those that believe him.[168]

MAGNIFYING THE LAW TO FULFILL THE LAW

Jesus Christ did not come to the earth to destroy the law, but rather to fulfill it.[169] Isaiah teaches that Christ magnified the law, saying *"He will magnify the law."*[170] To magnify is to enlarge, as with a microscope. Using a microscope, you can see life forms that were previously unseen because they are enlarged. Jesus did the same enlarging of the law of Moses when He preached the Sermon on the Mount in Matthew. Concerning adultery in Matthew 5:27-32, Jesus magnified or enlarged the unseen, root problem of adultery, when He revealed a previously unseen life form causing it—the spirit of lust. Jesus taught that imagining lustful adultery reaps the same guilt as committing the physical act. The spirit of lust is simply a fallen angel, or demon power, otherwise known as an evil spirit. The wisdom of Jesus enlarged the law so we can examine the root problem of adultery, which is the unseen, evil spirit of lust.

Thankfully, Christians can clean the inside of their cups, or their thought-lives, and be truly clean before the Lord. Conversely, the Pharisees cleaned only the outside of the cup and not the inside.[171] As we clean out our minds, bringing every thought into the obedience of Christ, we submit ourselves to

---

168 1 Timothy 4:16
169 Matthew 5:17
170 Isaiah 42:18-21
171 Luke 11:39

the law of the Spirit.[172] As a result, the Spirit quickens, or makes the Word of God live in our personal lives on a daily basis.[173]

Scripture teaches that you can fulfill all of the law through one powerful channel—love. Paul said you should owe only love to others and that love would fulfill all the law.[174] This love would not have been possible without the work of Jesus Christ on Calvary, as He shed His love upon us in the form of the Holy Ghost.[175] True love is the Holy Spirit, for the Holy Spirit is God, and God is love.[176]

Christians do not seek to destroy the Old Testament. Like Christ, believers see the magnification of the Old Testament laws and understand how the law of the Spirit helps them fulfill all righteousness and obedience in their daily lives.

CONCLUSION

The Holy Spirit always rightly divides the Word of truth in the mouth of *"two or three witnesses."* Faithful Bible teachers and students test all statements with Scripture, to find whether they are true, including blanket statements, creeds, and traditions of men—proving all things.[177]

Now that you know how the Holy Spirit rightly divides the Word of truth, you can begin looking into all Scripture to understand God's perfect will for your outward appearance, beginning with the four guidelines for modest clothing.

---

172 Romans 8:4
173 John 6:63, 2 Corinthians 4:16
174 Romans 13:8, Galatians 5:14
175 Acts 2:33, Romans 5:5
176 1 John 4:8
177 1 Thessalonians 5:21

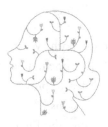

CHAPTER 3

Four Guidelines for Modest Clothing

"In like manner also, that women adorn themselves in modest apparel, with shamefacedness and sobriety; not with broided hair, or gold, or pearls, or costly array;"

—*1 Timothy 2:9*

How should a Christian dress in modest apparel? You may have wondered, "How do I know I have enough clothes on?" No doubt some Christians have struggled with the balance of wanting to look fashionable and modern, but not become seductive. Scriptures will give you confidence to know you are dressing in a way that honors God. People around you will know that you love the Lord Jesus Christ when you present yourself according to the modesty guidelines of the Bible.

MODESTY GUIDELINES

The clothes we wear are very important to God. Modest clothing is not a suggestion, as Paul commands Christians, specifically women, to wear modest clothing in 1 Timothy 2:9. Paul undoubtedly received the revelation about modest clothing from Jesus Christ, for he claims all his writings were inspired by Christ.[178] This further proves Jesus earnestly wants His followers to wear modest clothing.

---

178 Galatians 1:11-12

Modesty is a commandment for both women and men, as the Book of Genesis teaches. After Adam and Eve sinned, modest clothes were so important that God Himself came down to Eden to provide a sacrifice for their sins and to clothe them in "*coats*" or tunics of skins.[179]

We must stand for modesty because the Bible teaches it, just like we stand for the sanctity of life because God does. Teaching followers of Christ to observe the commandments of Christ is not legalism. It is being loyal to Jesus' commands, just as Jesus was loyal to all the Father's commands. In fact, ministers are actually fulfilling Jesus' Great Commission by teaching His disciples to observe the command for modest clothing, for Jesus admonishes His disciples to observe all His commandments.[180]

EVERY CHURCH WAS TAUGHT MODESTY

Every church Paul visited heard the same course of conduct,[181] including the command for modest clothing. Does your church teach modest clothing? It should! God loves unity among His churches. God knew that Christians would serve God best when they all had the same expectations and course of conduct.

Paul encouraged all Christians to have one faith, one mind, and walk in the same judgment.[182] Early Christians were of one heart and soul;[183] and before the second coming of Jesus Christ, all Christians will come to a unity of faith in the Word of God.[184] The true churches of Jesus Christ will be united on all of their teachings when Jesus returns, and modest clothing will be included in that group.

The apostle admonished the Philippians to all mind the same rule, or standard.[185] The Greek word for "rule" is "kanon" which means a carpenter's measuring tape or standard.[186] Every Christian should use the same standard, the Word of God, for measuring their lives.

---

179 Genesis 3:21
180 Matthew 28:20
181 1 Corinthians 4:17
182 Romans 12:16, 1 Corinthians 1:10, Ephesians 4:5
183 Acts 4:32
184 Ephesians 4:11-13
185 Philippians 3:16
186 *Voice of God Recordings Inc.*, "The Bible: Hebrew and Greek Lexicons," www.branham.org/en/messagesearch

REDIRECTING ATTENTION TO CHRIST

Two dictionary definitions of "modest" are "not revealing or emphasizing the figure" and "dressing to avoid indecency, especially to avoid sexual attention."[187] A person who dresses modestly tries to redirect the attention from themselves to someone else, our Lord and Savior, Jesus Christ. Christians should be humble, meaning that they should have a modest opinion of themselves as they consider their weaknesses, faults, and tendency to fail. They should be so impressed with the strength, righteousness, and prevailing power of Christ that they willingly redirect all attention to their Lord.

Just as all institutions and businesses have guidelines, or a course of conduct, God's kingdom has its guidelines. Modest clothing guidelines provide protection, boundaries, assurance, and safety. You have probably seen school children wearing uniforms or sports teams clothed identically. Their outward appearance helps you identify their cause, purpose, and mission. The same is true with Christians: their modest clothes proclaim their mission to magnify and glorify the Lord Jesus Christ.

Best of all, when you choose to dress modestly in obedience, the Holy Spirit gives you the invaluable, blessed assurance that you desire in your daily life. You will feel pure in your soul! Peter says obedience produces a feeling of a purified soul. He wrote, *"Seeing ye have purified your souls in obeying the truth through the Spirit unto unfeigned love of the brethren, see that ye love one another with a pure heart fervently."*[188] Paul says there are three parts to your being: mind, body, and soul.[189] Your mind and body may not feel pure, as the mind is the battlefield of good and evil thoughts, but your soul will feel clean from your obedience.

DEFINING PARTS OF THE BODY BY THE BIBLE

In Daniel chapter 2, the Bible provides a five-part division of the human body we can use as an outline to help us understand boundaries for each body area. Daniel was allowed by God to see and interpret Nebuchadnezzar's dream of

---

187 *English Oxford Living Dictionaries*, www.en.oxforddictionaries.com/definition/legalism
188 1 Peter 1:22
189 1 Thessalonians 5:23

the *"great image"* that represented the Times of the Gentiles.[190] Led of God, Daniel saw God's division of the image's body into five parts: the head, the breast and arms, the belly and thighs, the legs, and the feet (See Figure 2). This God-ordained division of the human image defines the five different areas of the body.

Figure 2

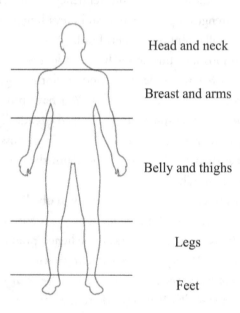

First, the head division would include the head and neck, with the lower boundary being the shoulder. Next, the breast and arms would include the area from the shoulder down to the bottom of the rib cage. Third, the belly and thighs would begin under the ribs and continue down to the knee. This region includes the area referred to in Scripture as the *"loins,"* which is the hips and reproductive area. Fourth, the legs are the area from the shin down to the ankle. Last, the foot division entails the area from the ankle down to the toes.

With these five divisions in mind, God in His mercy has given us a clear upper and lower boundary for our bodies that He wants us to cover with cloth-

190 Daniel 2:31

ing. As a rule of thumb, Christians should cover from the shoulders down to the shins, or put another way using the five-divisions Bible terminology, from the breast and arms down past the belly and thighs. The upper boundary must be the shoulder because exposed breasts can arouse lustful thoughts.[191] The shin, or upper-leg area below the knees, is the lower boundary because exposed thighs and loins are *"nakedness,"*[192] undoubtedly inciting lustful thoughts, whether a person is seated or standing.

FOUR GUIDELINES FOR MODEST CLOTHING

The Bible defines the perfect will of God on how to dress modestly. Over time and through much study, God revealed to me that there are four guidelines (though possibly more) Christians should honor concerning their outward appearance:

- Cover nakedness
- Thick clothing or multiple layers
- Gender-specific clothing
- Loose clothing

#1 GUIDELINE: COVER NAKEDNESS

The first guideline is to cover all areas of the body that God considers nakedness. The Scriptures that teach this guideline are Genesis 3:7, 21, Isaiah 47:1-3, 1 Kings 18:46, and Proverbs 31:17.

In Genesis 3:7 and 21, God provides the upper and lower boundaries for modest clothing: the shoulder and shin. Chapter 1 covers God's own choice for clothing in the section titled "The Beginning and Ending of Modest Clothing." Just as the unchanging God clothed Adam and Eve with modest, full-length tunics, we are sure He wants us clothed so that our breasts, belly, loins, thighs, and knees are fully covered.

In Isaiah 47:1-3, Isaiah told the *"virgin daughter of Babylon,"* or people in the city of Babylon, that God would allow their *"nakedness"* to be uncovered.

---

191 2 Samuel 11:2, Proverbs 5:19, Song of Solomon 7:6-8
192 Isaiah 47:2-3

In this case, nakedness meant uncovered thighs, or the area from the hips down to the knee. Thighs are clearly defined as one of the five divisions of the human body and Christians should always wear clothes that cover their thighs and knees.

1 Kings 18:46 and Proverbs 31:17 prove that the lower boundary for modest clothing is the shin. When Elijah ran to Jezreel, he girded up his loins, meaning he gathered up the end of his loose robe, which probably extended to his feet, and tucked it in to his belt, or girdle, so he could freely run. By girding up his loins, Elijah would have exposed his feet, ankles, and shins—but not his thighs. The same idea is seen for women in Proverbs 31:17, as the distinguished Proverbs 31 woman *"girdeth her loins with strength."* At times, Israeli men and women had to gird up their loins to do physical labor, exposing their shins, but were still able to cover the nakedness of their thighs. It is important to note that unless Israelis were involved in physical labor, they spent the rest of their time with their robes untucked from their girdles, presenting a more modest appearance that covered nearly all their legs.

MORE SUPPORT FOR COVERING THE SHOULDERS, BREASTS, LOINS, AND LEGS

There is much more Scriptural support for covering the body from the breasts (shoulders) down to the upper-leg (shins), as Figure 3 illustrates. I will start at the top of the body and work my way down.

Figure 3

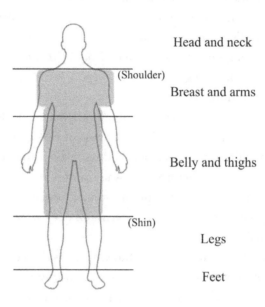

Some people may wonder if the shoulders should be covered. Exposing the shoulders is nakedness in the sight of God based upon the definition of the tunic in Genesis 3:21—"a long, shirt-like garment." An ancient tunic would certainly have covered the shoulders, as there are no Scriptures that support exposing shoulders in public.

Scripture proves exposing the breast or bosom area is considered nakedness. The breasts of a woman are strictly accessible and visible to her lawful husband only.[193] Whoredom, either adultery or fornication, is committed when anyone other than her husband presses or handles the breast of a woman.[194] Women should wear clothes that cover their breasts, and the rest of the body parts considered nakedness because Jesus taught that men are often tempted to look upon women and lust with sexual desires in their hearts.[195] If these sexual sins, whether committed in the mind or body, are unconfessed, those guilty will not inherit the Kingdom of God and will burn in the lake of fire.[196]

193 Proverbs 5:18-20, Hebrews 13:4
194 Ezekiel 23:3, Hosea 2:2
195 Matthew 5:27-28
196 1 Corinthians 6:9-10, Revelation 21:8

Additionally, there are 75 Scriptures in the King James Bible that reference the shoulders and none of them teach that exposing the shoulders is a godly act. The Israeli high priest is an example of covering the shoulders, as he wore a garment called an ephod, an apron-like garment, which completely covered his shoulders before going into the presence of God.[197] This ephod was worn on top of the longest tunic-like garment, the *"robe,"*[198] which covered the shoulders and extended to the feet.

God expresses that the uncovered loins and thighs are nakedness. The Lord instituted holy garments to cover the nakedness of the regular Israeli priests during acts of worship in the tabernacle and temple.[199] God commanded the priests to wear breeches to cover from the waist to the thighs, which were worn under the long, outer robe. As the priest ascended the elevated brazen altar, worshippers may have seen the linen breeches under the priest's robe rather than the priests' nakedness.[200]

The legs are not an area of nakedness but Christians should wisely choose to cover more of their legs, more of the time. While both Israeli men and women covered their legs, one Bible Almanac writes that Israeli women's robes always covered more of their legs than men, as women usually covered all of their legs, including the ankles and feet.[201] When physical work needed done, both men and women girded their loins and God allowed their shins to be exposed for short periods of time. The section "Ancient Hebrew Clothing" in Chapter 7 elaborates on traditional Hebrew clothing.

The Book of Revelation gives evidence that all of our legs will be covered in heaven, as Jesus Christ's garment covered His breast and arms and extended all the way to His feet. Revelation 1:13 says, John, the disciple whom Jesus loved,[202] saw a vision of Jesus in His glorified body, representing Christ's Supreme Deity. Jesus was clothed in a garment down to the foot. The Greek Lexicon defines garment as "reaching to the feet, ankles."[203] Observe first that Jesus was not

---

197 Exodus 28:6-12
198 Exodus 28:4
199 Exodus 28:42
200 Exodus 28:42-43
201 Packer, J.I. *Bible Almanac.* Nashville: Thomas Nelson, 1980.
202 John 21:20
203 *Voice of God Recordings Inc.*, "The Bible: Hebrew and Greek Lexicons," www.branham.org/en/messagesearch

showing off toned, muscular arms, abs, legs and thighs, like many do today. He was not showing off any body part. Jesus was clothed modestly.

The lesson is that Jesus Christ Himself will set the example for modest clothing in heaven. Jesus is the *"Great Shepherd"* according to Hebrews 13:20. He leads the way for the sheep to follow. Jesus, as a Man, models complete modesty and holiness in the clothing He wears throughout eternity. What a blessing it is to know that God delights in modesty standards in this world and in the eternal world to come!

APPLICATION

To apply the "cover nakedness" guideline, common sense tells you that exposing your breasts down to your thighs incites lustful thoughts in others. Remember to cover from your shoulders to your shins—which is the minimum. God's Spirit convicts me to cover all my legs, down to my ankles. For myself, a man, God calls me to spiritually lead my family and the church I pastor, so I lead in modesty as well. My clothing always covers from my shoulders down to my ankles. I never wear shorts because they would expose my thighs. All my pants reach at least to my ankles.

Although Christians do not wear robes today—the Bible does not command us to wear robes—we must still cover the same "real estate," or body divisions that God considers nakedness.

#2 GUIDELINE: THICK CLOTHING OR MULTIPLE LAYERS

The second guideline is to wear thick, opaque clothing or multiple layers of clothes in order to redirect attention away from your body. The Scriptures that teach this guideline are Genesis 3:21, Matthew 5:40, Judges 3:16, and John 21:7.

Genesis 3:21 teaches that God clothed Adam and Eve with coats of skins. These skins were probably lamb skins, since it would fit God's nature to have the first animal sacrifices foreshadow the crucifixion of Jesus Christ, Who is the *"Lamb of God"* Who takes away the sin of the world.[204]

204 John 1:29

If this was the case, a lamb-skin tunic would be very thick. This apparel would not reveal the form of the body, nor would it be see-through, making it very modest. An easy example of the thickness of this type of clothing is to picture in your mind shearling or sheepskin boots. God wanted thick clothing that did not reveal the form or private parts of the body. God's fashion choices are so different from modern fashions!

Layers of clothing are mentioned by Jesus in Matthew 5:40, in which our Lord spoke of one person owning both coats and cloaks. In Jesus' time, people needed multiple layers of clothes to keep warm during the cold conditions. The coats Jesus spoke of were thin, shirt-like undergarments, like tunics, worn next to the skin. These coats were the undergarment layer, like underwear today, but with much more cloth or material than our modern day underwear because tunics were like a very long shirt. The cloak was the outer garment, or outside garment, worn on top of the tunic or coat. Another word for cloak is "robe," which is like the scarlet robe the Roman soldiers put upon Jesus.[205] This robe or cloak was an "outer garment usually worn over the tunic."[206]

Judges 3:16 provides another example of these two layers—coats and cloaks. Ehud, the Israeli deliverer, hid a dagger under his outer garment by girding it to his right thigh. Girding the dagger meant binding or securing it in place using a belt, or girdle. Ehud's dagger was hidden from the evil Moabite king, Eglon, because it was under his outer raiment, or cloak.

It is important to state that God considered a person to be "naked" when he took off his outer garment—his cloak or robe. Without the outer garment, the person would be viewed in only his thin, tunic-undergarment. While fishing, Peter had his outer garment off, the "*fisher's coat*," and the Bible records Peter as being "*naked.*"[207] The reason Peter was not sinning, though, was because he was among men only—the other apostles. Jesus did a similar thing when He laid aside His garments before washing the apostles' feet.[208] Both Peter and Jesus did not sin, for they were not around women when they took off their outer garments during work (fishing) or worship (feet washing).

Some erroneously believe David danced naked in public before the Lord, but according to Scripture he wore at least two layers of clothing: a robe of fine

---

205 Matthew 27:28
206 *Voice of God Recordings Inc.*, "The Bible: Hebrew and Greek Lexicons," www.branham.org/en/messagesearch
207 John 21:7
208 John 13:4

linen and an ephod of linen.[209] David's wife Michal said he "*uncovered*" himself shamelessly in front of the handmaid servants.[210] Based upon the context, the only plausible meaning for "*uncovered*" is that David took off his royal clothing in order to be dressed in the same manner as the Levites, singers, and Chenaniah.[211] Nevertheless, the text proves Michal's accusation against David was wrong, for she died childless.[212] David, on the other hand, became more honored in his servants' eyes because he increased his rejoicing, dancing, and leaping before God![213]

APPLICATION

Applying the second guideline means wearing at least two layers or one thick layer of clothing, and abstaining from walking around in your underwear or undergarments in public. Appearing in public or at a pool or beach in a bathing suit would break God's Word, as most bathing suits and shorts only have one layer of thin clothing. Swimsuits almost always reveal the form of the body seductively, exposing areas of the body that God considers nakedness.

#3 GUIDELINE: GENDER-SPECIFIC CLOTHING

The third guideline is to wear gender-specific clothing, meaning men should wear men's clothing and women should wear women's clothing. The Scripture that directly teaches this guideline is Deuteronomy 22:5. Three more Scriptures support this guideline by emphasizing God's immutability and Jesus' example of not cross dressing: Malachi 3:6, Hebrews 4:15 and 13:8.

Although Deuteronomy 22:5 is an Old Testament Scripture, there are two reasons it applies to Christians. First, cross dressing is called an abomination, or disgusting thing, and no New Testament Scripture permits it. The reason Old Testament abominations remained detestable in the New is because God said He is unchanging.[214] His holy nature abhorred all evil, abominable acts

---

209 1 Chronicles 15:27
210 2 Samuel 6:20
211 1 Chronicles 15:27
212 2 Samuel 6:23
213 2 Samuel 6:22
214 Malachi 3:6

yesterday and abhors them today and will abhor them forever, for Jesus Christ is the same yesterday, today, and forever.[215] In the days of Moses and Jesus, men and women could be easily differentiated visually just by looking at their outer clothing, based upon Deuteronomy 22:5. Obedient, God-fearing Jews wore gender-specific outer garments, and so do Christians today.

Second, Jesus never cross-dressed like a woman. Hebrews 4:15 teaches that Jesus never broke one Old Testament commandment. Since cross dressing was strictly forbidden in the law of Moses, Jesus never wore clothes that pertained to a woman. Furthermore, Jesus instituted the New Testament and the Kingdom of God upon this earth while wearing men's garments. Jesus modeled and lived this standard during His earthly life. If Jesus is the same forever, then He will remain dressed like a man forever, throughout time and then into eternity.

Two other Bible references support the fact that God wants specific differences in the outward appearances of men and women. First, God commanded men to have short hair and women to have long, uncut hair.[216] This means men and women need different hair lengths *and* outer garments. Second, in king David's time, great emphasis was placed upon the virginity of the king's daughters, who wore garments of virginity.[217] While we find no record of virgin garments in the New Testament, this example shows that God's people always have a pattern of visually separating genders. God wants His society to operate with defined, God-given roles, easily determined by gender, outer garments, and hair length.

When a society allows gender and clothing to become indistinguishable, a state of confusion, or "Babel," occurs, and God is not the author of confusion.[218] In 2015 when Bruce Jenner publicly declared himself transgender and changed his name to Caitlyn, he was both "widely praised and heavily scrutinized."[219] According to Deuteronomy 22:5, God considers this transgender act an abomination, because a man, Bruce Jenner, is wearing the clothes of a woman. What most people do not realize, though, is that the same public scrutiny that Bruce Jenner received, partly for his cross dressing as a woman, was the same public scrutiny that women such as Marlene Dietrich and Katharine Hepburn received for wearing pants and dressing as men in the 1930s and 1940s—not

---

215 Hebrews 13:8
216 1 Corinthians 11:1-16
217 2 Samuel 13:18
218 1 Corinthians 14:33
219 "Caitlyn Jenner." *Encyclopedia Britannica*, www.britannica.com/biography/Caitlyn-Jenner.

even 100 years ago. The book "Women in Pants," by Catherine Smith and Cynthia Greig, fully documents the undeniable history of the scrutiny that surrounded women who first began cross dressing and wearing men's pants.

APPLICATION

Based upon America's Judeo-Christian foundation, American men should always wear pants and women should always wear dresses or skirts without compromise—at all times and in all situations. Other nations may have different types of clothes that pertain to gender.

For nearly 200 years our country honored the gender-specific clothing guideline, but acceptance for cross dressing became popular in the 1960s and 1970s, as Chapter 6 details.

#4 GUIDELINE: LOOSE CLOTHING

The fourth guideline is to wear loose clothing, as taught in Genesis 3:21, 1 Kings 19:13, Mark 16:5, Revelation 6:11, 7:14, and Proverbs 7:10.

In Genesis 3:21 and 1 Kings 19:13, the outer garments—coats for Adam and Eve, and a mantle for Elijah—were loose-fitting garments. As previously taught, Adam and Eve's animal-skin tunics were thick and long, but also loose-fitting. God never asked anyone to wear tight clothing, so loose clothes are His unchanging, holy pattern. Elijah's mantle was undoubtedly loose, as he could not have wrapped a skin-tight mantle around his face since robe materials, like linen and camel hair, are not stretchy.

The entire heavenly host of angels wear loose-fitting robes. Mark 16:5 describes the angel's attire on resurrection morning as a "*long, white garment.*" The Greek Lexicon defines "garment" as "a loose outer garment for men extending to the feet."[220]

Loose, long clothing is the will of heaven. In Revelation 7:14, multitudes of Christians who are washed in the blood of Jesus will also wear loose, white robes in heaven similar to those the angels wear. The word "robes" in Revelation 7:14 has the same Greek meaning as "garment" from Mark 16:5—"a loose

---

220 *Voice of God Recordings Inc.*, "The Bible: Hebrew and Greek Lexicons," www.branham.org/en/messagesearch

outer garment for men extending to the feet." It is clear that every person with eternal life will be clothed in loose, long, white robes for all eternity. If we are going to spend all eternity with loose clothes that cover our bodies, according to the wisdom and design of God Himself, then we should be happy to start wearing loose clothing right now. When you live your life here on earth according to the will of heaven, and wear loose, long clothing, you are letting the will of heaven come down to earth. This is a fulfillment of the Lord's prayer, "*Thy will be done in earth, as it is in heaven.*"[221]

Proverbs 7:10 speaks of a harlot or prostitute with an evil heart. She has the "*attire of an harlot.*" Even in the Old Testament days, certain garments pertained to harlots, as Genesis 38:14-19 speaks of in reference to Tamar. According to God's truth that there is nothing new under the sun,[222] harlots today, just like thousands of years ago, dress in a way that attracts the attention of men. Prostitutes are known for wearing tight, revealing clothing, breaking the Bible commands for loose clothing that also covers areas of the body God considers nakedness. From a logical standpoint, Christians must avoid wearing tight clothing because it draws the wrong kind of attention to the body.

APPLICATION

Christians should wear loose clothes at all times, not drawing sexual attention to themselves. God never asked anyone to wear tight outer garments, and He won't start now. Loose clothes make up both our earthly and heavenly wardrobes!

PUTTING YOUR CLOTHES TO THE TEST

Based upon these four modest clothing guidelines, you can now begin to recognize examples of immodest clothing and give your clothes the Word-test. You can keep the clothes that pass the four guideline test and send the immodest clothes to your local second-hand store.

To help you get started, I made a list of clothes that would most certainly be considered immodest according to the four Bible guidelines: mini-skirts,

---

221 Matthew 6:10
222 Ecclesiastes 1:9

sundresses, high-slit skirts, low-cut dresses, shorts, short-shorts, skinny jeans, yoga pants, halter or tube tops, sheer blouses, most swimsuits and bikinis, and tank-tops—just to name a few.

If you have a question about whether an article of clothing is modest, use the four guidelines to determine if the clothing is pleasing to God. If you feel the four guidelines still do not answer your question, then you should ask God to reveal His wisdom. While waiting for God's revelation from the Bible, you should refrain from wearing the questionable clothing until you can prove by Scripture that it is pleasing to God. Scripture declares that God seeks to give us abundant wisdom, but we must not doubt that God will provide the correct course of action, for doubt will lead us to missing the wisdom of God.[223] Refraining from wearing questionable clothes shows that you have patience, the fear the Lord, and a desire to please God more than men. Ask God for patience, for in patience you will possess your soul and have need of nothing.[224]

CONCLUSION

The Bible declares that its words are inspired of God and are profitable for doctrine, reproof, correction, and instruction that the Christian may be complete and furnished unto every good work.[225] In regards to the four guidelines for modest clothing, a sufficient amount of Scripture provides us with an unwavering doctrinal stand upon the witnesses of Holy Writ. Through nearly two decades of Bible study, I have never found the Bible supporting clothes that contradict the four guidelines. I have confidence in my Creator that His desire and command for modest clothing has never changed and never will.

It is possible that God may reveal to me a fifth or perhaps sixth guideline in the future. As I wait upon the Lord for further revelation, He will certainly renew my strength as the eagle.[226] God will empower me to run the Christian race without weariness, and walk without fainting.

I conclude this chapter in hope that you will now have an answer to anyone who asks you about the reason you choose to clothe yourself in such a modest, beautiful, but oftentimes, unpopular way. You can say with confidence, "God

---

223 Ephesians 1:8, James 1:5-7
224 Luke 21:19, James 1:4
225 2 Timothy 3:16-17
226 Isaiah 40:31

has four clearly defined guidelines for modest clothing, and I am following His commands in meekness and fear."

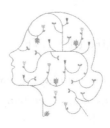

CHAPTER 4

Hair Length

"But if a woman have long hair, it is a glory to her: for her hair is given her for a covering."

—*1 Corinthians 11:15*

Just like men and women having separate garments, the Bible teaches that men and women should also have separate, distinct hair lengths. Scripture teaches that God requires women to keep their hair uncut and as long as genetically possible for their entire lives. God asks men to keep their hair cut short. When women obey the Word of God and keep their hair uncut, it is an honor to their husbands and to Christ. If men rebel against God and grow their hair out like a woman, they are considered shameful in the eyes of God.

NEW TESTAMENT TEACHING

Five New Testament texts support men and women having separate, distinct hair lengths: 1 Corinthians 11:1-16, John 11:1-2, 12:1-8, Luke 7:36-50, and Revelation 9:8.

Furthermore, you cannot find a text in Scripture where God asked any godly woman, whether in the Old or New Testaments, to cut or trim her hair in any way. A question arises whether a woman can trim her split ends. The Bible-based answer is no, women must not even trim their split ends. Contrary to the false idea that trimming split ends makes hair healthier, healthy hair comes from a healthy diet and daily care. Scissors must not come upon any part of the hair of a faithful, obedient Christian woman.

THE MAIN TEXT ON HAIR LENGTH

The main New Testament text for teaching on hair length is 1 Corinthians 11:1-16. The truth about hair length has been lying in the Scripture for nearly 2,000 years. Churches may label this text as cultural, which implies that they do not have to obey its commands—but they are wrong for four reasons. First, Paul never said this text was for the Corinthians only. In fact, verse 16 says this custom was for all *"the churches of God"*—not just one. Second, the apostle never labeled hair length as an area of liberty as he did for observing holy days, eating meat, and drinking wine. Third, hair length is directly associated with God's design for male headship, as verse 3 details. Paul says headship is a universal principle that pertains to *"every man,"* not just Corinthian men. Fourth, the unchanging pattern for hair length that God has laid out through the entire canon of Scripture is vindication that all Christians should honor Paul's teaching.

In verses 1-2, Paul urged the Corinthians to continue to follow his ordinances because he was taught the gospel by Christ Himself, as validated in Galatians 1:11-12: *"But I certify you, brethren, that the gospel which was preached of me is not after man. For I neither received it of man, neither was I taught it, but by the revelation of Jesus Christ."*

Verse 3 describes the God-ordained headship for the entire universe: man is head over the woman, Christ is head over man, and God, the eternal, invisible Spirit, is head over Christ. This headship or order of leadership is important because it is reflected in hair length according to verses 4-6. Hair length is a God-ordained symbol of authority or leadership.

Verse 4 teaches that a man dishonors Christ if he covers his head, by letting his hair grow long, as verse 14 says it is a shame for a man to have long hair. Then in verse 5, Paul teaches that a woman dishonors her husband if she prays or prophesies with an uncovered head. An uncovered head is a head that has cut or trimmed hair upon it, since verse 15 says a woman's long, uncut hair is *"given her for a covering."* Because it is a shame for a woman to be shorn (short hair) or shaven (all hair cut off), let her be covered, as verse 6 details.

Please know that the covering of a woman is not a cap or veil, as seen worn by women from Amish, Mennonite, and other sects. A woman's true covering is not a man-made covering, but a covering made and designed by God—her uncut hair. There is no Scripture that says a "cap or veil is given her for a covering," but there is Scripture that says *"her hair is given her for a covering."*

Verses 7-12 explain why women should have long hair: they came out of man in the beginning, and were created for the man. Man was created first and is the God-ordained leader of the family and church. Long hair on a woman is the sign of her husband's authority over her, as this authority is taught throughout the Bible.[227]

In verses 13-16, Paul asked the Corinthians to judge themselves: is it comely or fit, for a woman to pray to God uncovered? Is it fit for a woman to pray with short hair or a shaved head? Of course the answer is no, it is not fit for a woman to pray to God with cut hair, for cut hair is a sign of rebellion against the authority of her husband. Next, Paul states that nature itself teaches that long hair on a man is a shame. Modern science says 40% of all men experience baldness,[228] so we can again see the infallible truth of the Bible that God allows nature to teach us that long, uncut hair on a man is a shame. Nearly half of the men in the world go bald. This should let everyone know that God does not want long hair on men!

Verse 15 contains the plain, concise truth about the true head covering for a woman. Paul states that if a woman has long hair, it is a glory to her because her hair was given to her for a covering. Her long, uncut hair is her covering, not a cap or veil or any other man-made covering.

Paul ends this portion of Scripture in verse 16 by answering the question he asked in verse 13: Is it fit for a woman to pray to God uncovered, with short hair or a shaved head? The apostle says, despite some being contentious about this topic of hair length, *"we have no such custom."* In other words, Christians Paul associated with had no practice of women praying to God with short hair; neither did any other of the churches of God. The churches of God in the days of Paul did not allow women to prophesy or pray to God with short, trimmed hair, nor men to pray to God with long, uncut hair.

Undoubtedly, Paul taught this doctrine of women having long, uncut hair in every church he visited, saying, *"For this cause have I sent unto you Timotheus, who is my beloved son, and faithful in the Lord, who shall bring you into remembrance of my ways which be in Christ, as I teach everywhere in every church."*[229]

---

227 Genesis 3:16, Ephesians 5:22-24
228 "Baldness." *Encyclopedia Britannica*, www.britannica.com/science/baldness.
229 1 Corinthians 4:17

WHAT LONG HAIR REPRESENTS TO GOD

Based upon the Bible word *"covering,"* a beautiful Scripture from the Old Testament gives us further understanding of what long hair on a woman represents. Isaiah 30:1 says, *"Woe to the rebellious children, saith the Lord, that take counsel, but not of me; and that cover with a covering, but not of my spirit, that they may add sin to sin."*

God wants us to know that a natural woman's *"covering"* or hair represents the covering of the spiritual woman, or church of the Lord Jesus Christ. This means that the godly wife and the godly church both have coverings that they must maintain with their consecrated lives. Figure 4 explains this in depth.

Figure 4

Natural Bride	Spiritual Bride
She has a covering, which is her uncut hair (1 Corinthians 11:15). Her uncut hair is a symbol that she is under the authority or leadership of her head, or her husband.	The church's covering is the Spirit of God (Isaiah 30:1), which wrote the Word of God (2 Peter 1:21). The presence of the covering, which is the anointing of the Holy Ghost, proves she is under the authority of her ruler, Christ Jesus, her Husband.
She has untrimmed, uncut hair (1 Corinthians 11:5-6). She does not cut off, or take away any part of her covering, which is her hair. The faithful bride submits to every word of her husband (Ephesians 5:24).	The church submits to and lives by every Word the Holy Spirit wrote, taking nothing away from the Word (Matthew 4:4, Revelation 22:18-19). This church will not trim off parts of the Bible or neglect preaching any truth of God, whether society agrees with it or not.
To cut her hair is to deny God glory in her life and deny her husband honor. She does not reject or cut even one hair on her head (1 Corinthians 11:5, 15).	To reject one word of the Bible is to deny Christ glory in her life. The true church progresses in their walk with God, from glory to more glory (2 Corinthians 3:18).

THE HAIR OF MARY, SISTER OF LAZARUS

The second and third texts describe Lazarus's sister, Mary, who anointed Jesus with ointment in the Gospel of John:

> *"Now a certain man was sick, named Lazarus, of Bethany, the town of Mary and her sister Martha. (It was that Mary which anointed the Lord with ointment, and wiped his feet with her hair, whose brother Lazarus was sick.)"*[230]
>
> *"Then took Mary a pound of ointment of spikenard, very costly, and anointed the feet of Jesus, and wiped his feet with her hair: and the house was filled with the odour of the ointment."*[231]

The Greek Lexicon says this pound of ointment was 12 ounces of fragrant oil.[232] Mary used her hair to wipe the precious feet of Jesus Christ to prepare Him for his burial. This undeniable witness helps prove that godly women in the days of Jesus did not cut their hair, because it would be impossible for a woman with short hair to wash the feet of Christ. Short, bobbed hair could not wrap around the feet of Jesus and act as a towel to clean and anoint those precious, holy feet.

THE FORGIVEN WOMAN AT SIMON'S HOUSE

A fourth text in Luke 7:36-50 is very similar to that of John 12:3, as Luke speaks of a woman *"which was a sinner"* who went into the house of Simon the Pharisee. She must have seen how Simon and his servants did not kiss Jesus or wash His feet upon His entrance, or anoint His head with oil. Being moved by her love for Christ as Savior, the woman ceased not to kiss His feet, anoint them with oil, wash them with her tears of repentance, and wipe them with the hairs of her head. This act of love caused Jesus to tell her plainly that her sins were forgiven.[233] Observe again that this forgiven woman could not have wiped

---

230 John 11:1-2
231 John 12:3
232 *Voice of God Recordings Inc.*, "The Bible: Hebrew and Greek Lexicons," www.branham.org/en/messagesearch
233 Luke 7:48

Jesus' feet with short, bobbed hair; she had to have long, uncut hair with years of growth in order to wipe the precious feet of the Lord Jesus Christ.

LOCUSTS WITH THE HAIR OF WOMEN

The fifth text is Revelation 9:8: *"And they had hair as the hair of women, and their teeth were as the teeth of lions."* This Scripture helps prove that God has specific, different hair lengths for men and women.

Revelation 9:8 is part of a striking portion of Scripture about the tribulation period, detailed in Revelation 9:3-10. Under the 5th trumpet during the tribulation, God will allow locusts to torment unbelievers and those who have rejected Jesus Christ as Lord and ruler of their lives.

One of the physical attributes of these locusts is that they have *"hair as the hair of women."*[234] We must ask ourselves, What is the *"hair of women?"* What style of hair do these locusts have? Society cannot define what the *"hair of women"* means, as many women have short hair and look like men. God's Word must define what *"hair of women"* means. Based upon Paul's teaching from 1 Corinthians 11:1-16, women's hair is long and uncut. The tormenting locusts had to have had long, uncut hair. It seems their job is to torment the Christ-rejecting people who willingly took the mark of the beast. But why?

It seems that God may be allowing these locusts to haunt the sinners because they have refused to honor many of God's commands. Obviously, they did not accept God's salvation, the baptism of the Holy Ghost, and even hair length. These rebellious, religious apostates allowed their women to bob their hair and dishonor their husbands and God's Word. They never taught against men growing their hair out long to look like women. These false teachers and their followers took away the glory of God, which was the long, uncut hair from the women. Allowing women to cut their hair shamed their husbands, and ultimately Christ. The only description worthy of their rebellion would be Ichabod, for the glory of the woman and of the man (God's symbol of submission and headship) was taken away from the people.[235] The preachers took away truth from the people and failed to preach the entire Holy Bible. As a result, both the speakers and hearers were worthy of the wrath of God.

---

234 Revelation 9:8
235 1 Samuel 4:21

HOW LONG DOES GOD WANT WOMEN'S HAIR?

One question that I have been asked repeatedly on my YouTube channel is, "How long does God want my hair to be?" The answer is as long as your hair can grow. There is no set length that God is asking women to achieve, such as 12 or 24 inches. God wants a woman to leave her hair uncut for the remainder of her life. God designed that a woman's genetics determines exactly how long her hair will be and He is pleased if her hair is 3 inches at it's full length, or 6 inches, or 12 inches, or longer. God is not asking for a specific length of hair. He is asking only for uncut hair as a symbol of her full obedience to her husband.

OLD TESTAMENT TEACHING ON HAIR LENGTH

In the Old Testament, just as in the New, you will again find the indisputable truth that God never asked a godly woman to cut her hair. I conclude that Paul's teaching from the New Testament is in complete harmony with God's desire for hair length in the Old Testament. God's desire for separate hair lengths for men and women remained unchanged from Genesis 1:1 to Revelation 22:21.

Some Bible readers may be familiar with the Nazarite vow from Numbers 6:1-21. Part of this vow was for the dedicated individual, a man in this case, not to cut his hair for a period of time. At the end of the vow, he would cut his hair. In this case, uncut hair was a sign of total consecration or dedication to God. I cannot find an example of a woman under a Nazarite vow, nor have I found a woman under a Nazarite vow ever cutting her hair, so it would seem that only men were to cut their hair at the conclusion of their Nazarite vow. It seems women, in terms of their hair, were under a lifelong Nazarite vow, meaning they were never to cut their hair. This lifelong dedication would be in complete harmony with God's command for women's hair length in the New Testament.[236]

According to Scripture alone, God has always asked all godly women, whether Jewish or Christian, to do the same—leave their hair uncut as a sign of total consecration or dedication to the plan of God for their lives. All Christian

---

236 1 Corinthians 11:1-16

women are under a similar total consecration to God not to cut their hair in order to display the symbol of headship.

Furthermore, as you read deeper in the Old Testament, there are two specific cases in which God did command the cutting of hair, but it was never a command given to godly, Jewish women, such as Sarah, Rebekah, Abigail, Esther, and the like. Therefore, these two examples do not pertain to consecrated Christian women today.

The first example is from Deuteronomy 21:10-13. Moses commanded that Israelite men were to have their new wives, taken from captivity after war with an enemy nation, shave their own heads as part of their transition into the Jewish religion and culture. Observe that the faithful, experienced Jewish women were never commanded to cut their hair in any manner.

The second example is from Jeremiah 7:28-30. God was speaking to Jerusalem, the capital of the nation of Israel, and upbraided them for their disobedience, rebellion, and abominable acts. God said, "*Cut off thine hair, O Jerusalem, and cast it away and take up a lamentation on high places; for the Lord hath rejected and forsaken the generation of His wrath.*" It is difficult to tell if God was speaking literally to every man and woman, or just men, or just women in this case. It is likely that this is simply figurative language in which God was speaking to the entire people rather than individuals. One thing is for sure, God told them to cut off their hair because He was rejecting and forsaking their generation due to their wickedness and abominable acts. So cutting hair in this case was a sign of being rejected by God. Similarly, a woman cutting her hair today is a shameful act and a sign that she is not submitting to her husband.

CONCLUSION

All the infallible Bible evidence concerning hair length proves that Christian men should frequently cut their hair so as not to bring shame upon themselves and their head, the Lord Jesus. Christian women should let their hair grow long and uncut for the rest of their consecrated walks with the Lord Jesus. Obedience will bring honor and glory to their husbands, and their spiritual husband, Jesus Christ.

God never asked an obedient, faithful, godly Jewish or Christian woman to cut her hair for the sake of fashion, convenience, style, or beauty, as some women believe they can today. All Christian women are to have long, uncut hair as a sign that they are under the headship of their husbands, Christ, and God. Living by these truths will keep the covering of the anointing of the Holy Ghost upon us, that the glory of God not depart from our homes and churches.

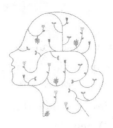

CHAPTER 5

Jewelry, Makeup, Tattoos, and High Heels

"I will praise thee; for I am fearfully and wonderfully made: marvellous are thy works; and that my soul knoweth right well."

—Psalm 139:14

In addition to modest clothing and hair length, four other areas of your outward appearance should be examined according to the Bible. This chapter will expound on the Bible's witnesses about the following accessories for your outward appearance: jewelry, makeup, tattoos, and high heels.

CHRISTIAN LIBERTIES

With the proper understanding of our Christian liberties, you can be sure you are walking in the faith and strengthening other believers' faith at the same time. Christian liberties can be defined as carnal, earthly actions that are not sins, but also do not make us more spiritual.[237] In other words, God gives us freedom of choice and we can either allow actions or disallow them. God does not give us freedom of choice in regards to makeup, tattoos and high heels, for each is contrary to Scripture. However there is some freedom of choice with certain types of jewelry.

Whether we allow or disallow liberties, our hearts must offer thanksgiving

---

237 1 Corinthians 8:8

unto our Lord Jesus Christ.[238] If you have any doubt that an action is not pleasing to God and cannot give God thanks during the action, you must abstain from it. Whatever is not done in faith is sin.[239] There are times that Christians should not display their liberties in public, but keep them private, between themselves and God alone.[240] When deciding whether or not to act upon a liberty, loving your neighbor should be your greatest concern. The Bible commands us to choose actions that please others rather than ourselves, as Jesus Christ modeled for us.[241]

Some texts that deal with Christian liberties are Romans 14:1-23, 1 Corinthians 8:1-13 and 10:14-33. In these texts, the specific examples of Christian liberties include foods,[242] observing holy days,[243] and wine.[244]

First, the food we eat is an area of Christian liberty, as some may choose to eat meat while others may eat only herbs or vegetables.[245] In Paul's time, the eating of meat was an issue, as believers in Corinth would find themselves in public and private settings where meat would be offered them to eat. If those serving the meat to the Christians expressed that the meat was offered in a sacrifice to idols,[246] the apostle urged believers to be aware that other, weaker believers may be watching them and thus it would be wise to refrain from eating the meat due to its connection to idolatry. The experienced believer knew that eating meat sacrificed to an idol would not have any impact upon his faith, for he could ignore the idolatry and give thanks to Christ for the food. But the weaker believer may be impacted by fear of the meat's connection to idolatry. The lesson is that we should not choose an action that will cause a weaker believer to stumble into sin, even if the action does not make us sin.

Next, observing holy days are days that Christians separate as more important days than others.[247] Paul stressed that no matter if a day is considered holy, every day should be a day to be thankful for. Some Christians might observe Jewish feast days or keep the Sabbath, but the apostle made it clear that these

---

238 Romans 14:6
239 Romans 14:23
240 Romans 14:22
241 Romans 15:1-3
242 Romans 14:2
243 Romans 14:5
244 Romans 14:21
245 Romans 14:2
246 1 Corinthians 8:4-13
247 Romans 14:5-6

observances were shadows of things to come and not the ultimate meaning, which was Christ.[248] The lesson is to respect others' convictions and be thankful that they are worshipping Jesus Christ.

Last, drinking wine is an area of Christian liberty according to Paul. As a guideline, Christians should abstain from all public and private alcohol consumption except in church communion services and for genuine medicinal needs.

The major concern with wine, as with meat offered to idols, is that we don't cause others to stumble into sin. Paul wrote that Christians may be offered to drink wine in public or in someone's home and would then have to be very cautious about who was watching them drink wine.[249] Paul teaches that any drink that has alcoholic content should not be consumed by a Christian in a public setting for the protection of the consciences of weaker Christians, who may see a Christian drinking wine and then go get drunk, eventually becoming apostate to Christianity due to drunkenness.[250] Recall that drunkards will not inherit the kingdom of God.[251] The conclusion is that wine should not be drank in public, except during a church communion service.[252]

The public use of wine was different in the days of Christ than it is today. Wine drank in public would either have been watered down or drank in very small amounts over long periods of time in order to avoid drunkenness, as evidenced in Jesus' first miracle.[253] Jesus was God in flesh, and God's unchanging standard condemns drunkenness from both testaments.[254] Jesus would not do a miracle that would lead people to committing the sin of drunkenness. Therefore, either the wine was watered down or the portions of wine that would be drunk at a long wedding reception were very small. Jesus' miracle of turning water into wine was a legitimate miracle, as the hand of God created the best quality of wine for latter part of the wedding reception. Yet we know God would not be pleased with a reception filled with drunks, for His Word condemns drunkenness.

Today, public usage of wine is not as moderate as the days of Christ. Often

---

248 Colossians 2:16-17, Hebrews 10:1-22
249 1 Corinthians 10:25-33
250 Romans 14:21
251 1 Corinthians 6:10, Galatians 5:21
252 Luke 22:18-20, 1 Corinthians 11:17-34
253 John 2:1-11
254 Proverbs 20:1, Galatians 5:21

celebrations such as receptions and New Year's parties result in much drunkenness, with very little moderation. Therefore, a Christian should refrain from drinking in these public venues, that his liberty not become a stumbling block to weaker Christians who are watching his actions.

Furthermore, wine has become a major money-making industry in the United States and it seems that wine-tasting has taken on a hobby-mentality. People taste wine in public settings simply for the fun of intoxication and socialization. Some may use the excuse of needing to drink in order to be at peace while socializing, but Christians should look to Christ, Who *"is our peace."*[255] Christians should abstain from this frivolity, as we are called to be intoxicated with the Holy Ghost, and not natural wine or strong drink.[256]

Wine can be used in other ways. It is noteworthy that Paul recommended that Timothy use a little wine for his stomach's sake and often infirmities.[257] Wine can then be used as a medicine in certain cases but great efforts should be made to limit the use in order to avoid a habitual consumption that could lead to addiction.

While Christians should not judge each other about the liberties that they allow, we must judge ourselves that we are not causing others to stumble and fall into sin.[258] Paul is clear that a weak Christian can spiritually perish with a defiled conscience through the bad influence of another Christian who took his liberty too far and did not consider how his actions would affect another Christian.[259] In these cases, the Christian who took his liberty too far not only sinned against the weak Christian, but also sinned against Christ.[260] Because of this great responsibility that Christians have to lead godly lives in front of other Christians, Paul took the attitude that he would not eat meat as long as the world was standing in order that he would not cause another Christian to fall into sin.[261] Each of us must have the same attitude—we will abstain from any pleasurable Christian liberty for the rest of our lives if we know it may cause the stumbling of weaker Christians.

---

255 Ephesians 2:14
256 Ephesians 5:18
257 1 Timothy 5:23
258 Romans 14:13-15
259 1 Corinthians 8:7-11
260 1 Corinthians 8:12
261 1 Corinthians 8:13

JEWELRY

While the three examples of liberties above are clearly defined—food, observing holy days, and wine—a case can be made for other areas of liberty. Wearing jewelry seems to be a liberty because the Bible provides examples of godly people wearing jewelry. Ungodly people also wear jewelry, so jewelry-wearing is not one sided.

The Bible contains numerous references to jewelry and it is clear that wearing certain types of inexpensive jewelry, in moderation, is acceptable to our Lord. Four guidelines ensure a believer's jewelry-wearing honors God: spending little time on jewelry, avoiding expensive jewelry, wearing few pieces of jewelry, and wearing jewelry with a godly message.

First, a Christian must spend little time adorning herself with jewelry. More emphasis must be placed on her inward adorning than the outward, as Paul pleaded that women adorn themselves in shamefacedness and sobriety rather than costly array of gold and pearls.[262] Shamefacedness is not a word we use much today, but it means to have a "sense of honor" and "bashfulness, reverence, and regard for others."[263] Similarly, sobriety means self control. The context of Paul's teachings about modest adorning show that women must exhibit self control in everything they wear. Our Christian sisters must be adorned with an attitude of honor and regard for others—especially a regard for men, who are often tempted through the lust of the eyes.

Second, Paul and Peter teach that expensive jewelry should be avoided.[264] What is valuable in the sight of God and of a great price for Christian women is a meek, quiet, and submissive attitude.[265] Flaunting wealth is ultimately fleeting, prideful, and vain in light of eternity.[266]

Third, the amount of jewelry worn should be minimal. Paul teaches "sobriety,"[267] meaning self control in the Greek.[268] The haughty, prideful daughters

---

262 1 Timothy 2:9
263 *Voice of God Recordings Inc.*, "The Bible: Hebrew and Greek Lexicons," www.branham.org/en/messagesearch
264 1 Timothy 2:9, 1 Peter 3:3
265 1 Peter 3:4-5
266 Proverbs 6:16-17, 23:5, 1 Timothy 6:7
267 1 Timothy 2:9
268 *Voice of God Recordings Inc.*, "The Bible: Hebrew and Greek Lexicons," www.branham.org/en/messagesearch

of Zion lacked sobriety, and wore 21 different outward accessories,[269] ranging from feet ornaments to bonnets for their heads. God assured those women that all their attempts to look beautiful would backfire and their end would be a burning destruction and desolation.[270] Additionally, along with the amount of jewelry worn, Christians should practice moderation in all things.[271]

Fourth, jewelry must carry a godly message. Any jewelry with wicked, devilish symbols, worldly images, or foul language does not please God and thus should be avoided at all times. Whatever we do, say, or wear, should glorify our Lord and Savior, Jesus Christ. *"And whatsoever ye do in word or deed, do all in the name of the Lord Jesus, giving thanks to God and the Father by him."*[272]

Scripture verifies the types of jewelry God accepts: rings,[273] necklaces,[274] and bracelets.[275]

RINGS

Christians can wear some rings that are acceptable unto God. The Biblical pattern for acceptable rings is that they have a meaningful purpose, such as in the cases of Mordecai, Joseph, and the prodigal son. These rings all symbolized authority and were used in sealing official documents. Mordecai received a signet ring from King Ahasuerus when he was given the power and authority of Haman's former position.[276] Joseph, son of Jacob, was given a ring to wear when he was exalted to second in command in Egypt.[277] Even our Lord Jesus' parable of the prodigal son included a ring being placed upon his finger once he was restored to his family.[278]

Today, Christians are most likely to wear wedding rings to symbolize their unending vows of marital faithfulness to their spouse. Wedding rings can be condemned in certain Christian circles, but there is no Scriptural evidence for this idea. Although Scriptures don't specifically support wedding rings, the

---

269 Isaiah 3:16-24
270 Isaiah 4:1-6
271 Philippians 4:5
272 Colossians 3:17
273 Genesis 41:42, Luke 15:22
274 Genesis 41:42, Proverbs 1:9, Song of Solomon 1:10
275 Genesis 24:22
276 Esther 8:2-3
277 Genesis 41:42
278 Luke 15:22

wearing of wedding rings is not forbidden. Since godly men wore rings with a purpose, wedding rings can be categorized as an area of Christian liberty because of their purpose, as long as they are not excessive or ostentatious.

NOSE RINGS

Nose rings are becoming more commonplace in American culture. The question is, "Are nose rings acceptable according to the Bible?" The answer is no for a couple of reasons.

First, nose rings pierce through the skin and shed blood, and the unchanging God never commanded His people to wear jewelry that shed blood, left permanent marks on their skin, or damaged their body in anyway. The bodies of Christians are likened to a holy temple and thus must be treated with reverence and not purposely damaged.[279] Your body is not your own. You are a temple of the Holy Ghost. Our God delights in our obedience to honor the bodies He has graciously created. God does not teach us to pierce our bodies, cause ourselves to bleed, or leave permanent marks on our bodies. No New Testament teaching permits believers to damage their bodies in any way.

Second, we do not have two or three witnesses that prove godly people wore nose rings. Nose jewels are alluded to in only one Scripture: Isaiah 3:21. As mentioned previously, this is a negative example of nose jewels because the prideful, seductive daughters of Zion, whose end was destruction and desolation, were adorned in 21 different accessories. God was not pleased with their vain, outward accessories. Some think Genesis 24:47 supports nose rings, but we have very little information about this event. Abraham's servant put an "*earring upon*" Rebekah's face at the time of her engagement to Isaac, but God has never asked His obedient people to pierce and permanently scar their bodies. Putting an earring upon her face was likely a custom for her engagement. This one isolated, ambiguous Scripture is not evidence for nose rings, because the rest of the Bible never teaches anyone to wear them.

---

[279] 1 Corinthians 3:17, 6:19

NECKLACES

The Bible offers support for the wearing of necklaces in moderation. Joseph and Solomon's bride wore necklaces as representations of their authority.[280] Necklaces were also used symbolically to represent the reward of obedience. If children faithfully obeyed the instructions and laws of their parents, the grace of God would be as a chain about their necks.[281] Therefore, necklaces can be categorized as an area of Christian liberty, as long as they follow the four guidelines listed above.

BRACELETS

Bracelets may also be worn in moderation, as they were worn by Rebekah upon her engagement to Isaac.[282] God Himself, in an allegory of His rescuing and adorning of Israel, put bracelets upon the hands of His bride.[283] Bracelets are an area of Christian liberty, as long as they follow the four guidelines listed above.

EARRINGS

Earrings should be avoided at all times because the negative witnesses in Scripture greatly outweigh the positive. Out of 11 Biblical texts about earrings, seven passages describe their usage in negative terms. Conversely, two Scriptural portions use earrings allegorically in positive terms. The final two reference earrings in ambiguous terms. Additionally, modern day earrings require piercing, bleeding, and scarring of the body, which God never ordained for His obedient people.

In Genesis 35:1-4, God commanded Jacob to return to Bethel and build an altar of worship. Knowing this, Jacob commanded that his family bury all their idols and earrings under an oak tree in Shechem. It seems Jacob's family had to bury all idols that they worshipped, which included false idols and the fashion

---

280 Genesis 41:42, Song of Solomon 1:10
281 Proverbs 1:9
282 Genesis 24:22
283 Ezekiel 16:11

of wearing earrings, before appearing before the living God at the house of God.

A second negative witness is the Israelites' use of earrings after the exodus out of Egypt. In the absence of Moses, the backslidden, idolatrous Israelites broke off their earrings at the command of Aaron in order to build the golden calf, which God abhorred.[284] Israel received these earrings from the Egyptians during the exodus.[285] God's purpose, though, was not for Israel to wear the earrings, but to use them to help build the tabernacle in the wilderness.[286] Later in their exodus journey, their armies obtained earrings as spoils of war and they dedicated them to the tabernacle of the Lord as an oblation and memorial.[287] Earrings never became a part of their daily lives.

A third negative witness involved Gideon's interactions with the Ishmaelites in Judges 8:22-27. The Ishmaelites possessed golden earrings, but not Israel. Rather than rule over the Ishmaelites, Gideon requested and received their earrings and formed an ephod that later became an object of idolatry in Israel.

Isaiah and Hosea record a fourth and fifth negative witness about earrings. In both contexts, God's two prophets recorded that earrings were a hindrance to women as a source of pride and lustful seduction.[288] Likewise, some women today still use earrings as tool of pride and seduction.

Exodus 21:6 and Deuteronomy 15:17 provide the sixth and seventh negative witnesses about earrings. In these texts, you will read about earrings called "*auls*" in the King James Version. Auls were permanent earrings given to Jewish slaves who purposely rejected freedom and wanted to remain slaves forever. The purpose behind the aul was to leave a permanent mark on the ears of the Jewish slaves so that their choice to be a slave for life would be instantly seen by all. These slaves ultimately rejected their God-given inheritance, which included the land of their forefathers. Auls were visible signs of the judgment of God upon unbelieving, faithless Israelites.

Imagine you lived in the days of Moses and saw slaves with auls in their ears. The permanent, visible auls immediately identified who was enslaved. The free Israelites would not have worn similar earrings to those of the slaves, for God

---

284 Exodus 32:2-3
285 Exodus 3:21-22, 12:35-36
286 Exodus 35:22
287 Numbers 31:48-54
288 Isaiah 3:20, Hosea 2:13

has always distinguished between holy and unholy.[289] God is not the author of confusion. He ordered every part of Jewish life. Their outer garments and hair length revealed their gender. Their ears revealed their choice of freedom or slavery. The Biblical pattern for earrings, then, shows that Jewish slaves and heathens used piercings. God's people may have possessed earrings as customary engagement gifts, for currency or barter, but not for everyday wear.

Christians should not have their ears pierced because piercing does not fit the unchanging character of God. Use the "Honor Your Body" guideline: no piercing our bodies, no deliberately causing ourselves to bleed, and no leaving permanent marks on our bodies. No New Testament teaching allows Christians to break the "Honor Your Body" guideline.

Proverbs 25:12 and Ezekiel 16:12 give two positive, allegorical witnesses for earrings. Proverbs describes a golden earring as representing a wise judge speaking to an obedient listener, with the emphasis on the value of hearing wise counsel—not on outward adornment. In Ezekiel, God Himself said He adorned Israel with earrings, which represents Israel's obedience to God's wise counsel. Both of these examples are allegorical and not literal, in contrast to the seven literal examples of earrings being described in a negative way.

Two other portions of Scripture are ambiguous about the use of earrings: Rebekah's engagement[290] and Job's restoration.[291] Both Rebekah and Job were given earrings as gifts, but we are not told what they did with them. It seems Rebekah's earrings were given to her as part of an engagement custom and not as an everyday accessory. Moreover, consider that her relatives in the next generation, Jacob's family, were commanded to bury their earrings before presenting themselves before God in His provided place of worship, Bethel. The idea of earrings as an engagement gift and not an everyday accessory also connects back to God's adorning of His engaged spouse, Israel.[292]

Job received an earring from each of his friends after God restored his health and family in Job 42:11. We cannot presume that God wanted Job to walk around daily, wearing multiple earrings, especially since we know the haughty daughters of Zion wore 21 different accessories that manifested their prideful, lustful hearts. Furthermore, we know God is more interested in the inward

---

289 Leviticus 20:26
290 Genesis 24:30
291 Job 42:11
292 Ezekiel 16:11

adornment than the outward. This story of Job provides more support that earrings were used by the followers of God as gifts of custom, and perhaps for currency and barter, rather than for everyday wear.

MAKEUP

Not in one Scripture does God command any woman or man to wear makeup, or paint their face in anyway. If God wanted His daughters to wear makeup, or "*paint*," as the King James Version describes it, He would have told them to do so in His Word. God's nature and His simple, humble design for the physical appearance align. His focus is on the inner man, while outward beauty is vain.[293] God wants us to present our clean, natural faces to others because God created our faces and said our entire bodies were "*fearfully and wonderfully made*," even "*marvelous.*"[294] According to the psalmist, no makeup can improve or make more beautiful the face that God already created for each of us. "*For thou hast possessed my reins: thou hast covered me in my mother's womb. I will praise thee; for I am fearfully and wonderfully made: marvellous are thy works; and that my soul knoweth right well.*" These Scriptures help women overcome all feelings of insufficiency. Women don't have to hide behind makeup because Christ assures their identity is found in Him.

Makeup is a superficial and false covering that God did not intend to be added to His creation. It's a shame that advertisers and Hollywood have convinced millions that the faces God made for them are not good enough. The truth is that your face is best just the way God made it and you can rejoice in the true face God gave you. We shouldn't desire a false appearance since the Bible says that charity, or love, rejoices in the truth.[295] Love doesn't rejoice in a false, superficial covering, but it does rejoice in a true, natural appearance.

Three Scriptures teach Jewish and Christian women to abstain from wearing makeup: 2 Kings 9:30, Jeremiah 4:30, and Ezekiel 23:40. The entire rest of the Bible can be added to this list because no Scriptures command any woman, whether godly or ungodly, to paint her face or wear any facial cosmetic.

Jezebel, wife of Ahab, painted her face in 2 Kings 9:30. She was likely the

---

293 Proverbs 31:30
294 Psalm 139:13-14
295 1 Corinthians 13:6

most evil woman in the entire Bible. She murdered God's faithful prophets and by usurping her husband's authority, greedily ordered the murder of an innocent man named Naboth.[296] Jezebel devoutly worshipped idols, such as Baal,[297] and practiced whoredoms and witchcraft.[298]

Jezebel is the only woman recorded in the Bible as painting her face, as the other two examples of women painting their faces were nations depicted as immoral women. Out of over 440 references to the "face" in the Bible, only Jezebel is named as one who used facial cosmetics. Jezebel, an idol worshipper, was a heathen in the sight of God, Who commanded Israel to learn not the ways of the heathen.[299] At the end of her life, Jezebel's response to the news of Jehu's coming was to paint her face in rebellion to the God of Israel, which led to her swift judgment. Without a doubt, face-painting, facial cosmetics, and makeup are linked to heathenism and idolatry according to Jezebel's behavior in the Bible and history itself, which Chapter 6 covers.

What may come as a surprise is that Jesus prophesied that this same spirit of Jezebel would return and seduce Christians in the New Testament dispensation.[300] We must be cautious of women in the Christian church who act like Jezebel by usurping authority over men, silencing the voices of true preachers, acting greedily, seducing followers into idolatry, and even painting their faces with makeup. Through a simple study of famous modern televangelists, we can quickly find examples of women who preach, wear makeup, emphasize money and prosperity, and allow their followers to participate in sinful, idolatrous indulgences. If you currently follow a woman with the Jezebel spirit, repent, and cry out to God for His leadership in finding a true church that possesses the Spirit of God. When the prophet Elijah found himself threatened by the wicked Jezebel, he ran into the wilderness, was fed by God, and was made aware of the 7,000 other believers who had not bowed down to the Jezebel religion. If you seek God, crying out to Him, He will lead you to other believers who want to worship Christ in Spirit and in truth!

The next Scriptural witness, Jeremiah 4:30, shows God speaking through the prophet Jeremiah to all of Israel around 600 B.C. The Lord gave the following message to Israel at the time of one of the punishments for committing

---

296 1 Kings Chapters 18, 21
297 1 Kings 18:19
298 2 Kings 9:22
299 Deuteronomy 30:16-17, Jeremiah 10:2
300 Revelation 2:20

wickedness and rebellion against Him: *"And when thou art spoiled, what wilt thou do? Though thou clothest thyself with crimson, though thou deckest thee with ornaments of gold, though thou rentest thy face with painting, in vain shalt thou make thyself fair; thy lovers will despise thee, they will seek thy life."*[301] This Scripture shows that it is vanity to wear expensive clothing and use makeup. Peter presents a similar message in the New Testament, saying a woman's inner beauty and spiritual adornment of a meek and quiet spirit is a great value in God's sight.[302]

Jeremiah chapter 4 is a picture of God issuing a sentence of destruction upon Judah and Jerusalem through horsemen and bowmen.[303] Though not a final destruction, Israel was being punished for their evil doings, bitter wickedness, rebellion, and foolishness.[304] God then speaks in verse 30 that Israel's *"lovers"* will despise her and seek to kill her despite her efforts to wear expensive clothing, ornaments, and have a painted face. Notice that Israel was not painting her face to please God, for God never asked any woman to wear facial cosmetics. Israel was painting her face to please her idols and the nations that taught her their heathen ways. Sadly, God's people then were doing the same thing Jezebel did a few hundred years earlier—painting their faces in the day of their destruction!

The last Scripture about makeup is found in Ezekiel 23:40, which was probably spoken near the same time as Jeremiah spoke his prophecy of destruction. Ezekiel's audience was most likely Jews in Babylon due to their exile from the Promised Land. The entire chapter of Ezekiel 23 portrays Israel as an adulterous woman who lusts after the gods of other nations, such as Egypt and Assyria.[305] In verses 40-41 and 43-44, Ezekiel says: *"And furthermore, that ye have sent for men to come from far, unto whom a messenger was sent; and, lo, they came: for whom thou didst wash thyself, paintedst thy eyes, and deckedst thyself with ornaments, And satest upon a stately bed, and a table prepared before it, whereupon thou hast set mine incense and mine oil. Then said I unto her that was old in adulteries, Will they now commit whoredoms with her, and she with them? Yet they went in unto her, as they go in unto a woman that playeth the harlot: so went they in unto Aholah and unto Aholibah, the lewd women."*

301 Jeremiah 4:30
302 1 Peter 3:3-4
303 Jeremiah 4:3, 6, 12, 29
304 Jeremiah 4:4, 17, 18, 22, 27
305 Ezekiel 23:3, 4, 43-44

God likens Israel unto a woman who is receiving her adulterous lovers and gives details on how she prepares for her lovers—she washes herself, paints her eyes, or puts on makeup, then puts on ornaments and sits on a bed near a table prepared for a meal. This immoral, idolatrous woman was going to lure her lover with all the fleshly lusts, including his appetite, a decorated bed, and the visual seduction of makeup.

Based upon these three Scriptures—2 Kings 9:30, Jeremiah 4:30, and Ezekiel 23:40—God's Word is against the use of makeup and facial cosmetics. The entire rest of the Bible does not offer even one hint of God requesting facial cosmetics upon any man or woman. What God does want on our faces is His glory—the anointing of the Holy Spirit. The Bible says we behold His glory and become changed into His image, from glory to glory, by the Spirit of the Lord. Think of how much more spiritual glory could be presented to this lost and dying world if believers spent more time praying and seeking God for the salvation of souls rather than painting a false face upon their countenances. Let the glory of Jesus Christ be upon your face instead of makeup. *"But we all, with open face beholding as in a glass the glory of the Lord, are changed into the same image from glory to glory, even as by the Spirit of the Lord."*[306]

Numerous people have erroneously told me that Esther wore makeup but there is absolutely no Scriptural support for this belief. The Bible never says Esther painted her face, as it says for Jezebel and twice for Israel in allegories. Scripturally, Esther was purified using oils—not face painting. Esther 2:9 and 2:12 declare she was given *"things for purification,"* which were *"oils of myrrh"* and *"sweet odors."* Esther was most likely given moisturizing oils for topical skin care. Perhaps Esther's lack of makeup was the distinguishing characteristic that attracted the king to her inner beauty. Please do not be deceived by the gross misunderstanding among churches concerning Esther, as Scripture never states that she used makeup to paint her face. Do not be influenced by those who add to the Words of God, for they shall be found liars.[307] Keep God's commands, and live! *"He taught me also, and said unto me, Let thine heart retain my words: keep my commandments, and live."*[308]

---

306 2 Corinthians 3:18
307 Proverbs 30:5-6
308 Proverbs 4:4

TATTOOS

During my college days, I was greatly tempted to get a tattoo. I had already repented of my sins and was serving the Lord Jesus, but not with the knowledge or zeal that I have today. Many of my college friends were getting tattoos, and I wanted one that said "Jesus" above a cross and the words "My Refuge" under the cross. I was torn about the final decision, as I had felt a conviction to refrain from marking my body. So I decided to call my mother's pastor and his wife, and they pointed me to Leviticus 19:28. After opening my Bible and reading this for myself, the question was settled—no tattoo for me!

In Leviticus 19:28, the Lord God told Moses, *"Ye shall not make any cuttings in your flesh for the dead, nor print any marks upon you: I am the Lord."* Based upon this Scripture, tattoos are forbidden for Jews and Christians. Furthermore, tattoos are never commanded nor approved of in the New Testament. The pattern of our Holy God is the "Honor Your Body" guideline—that humans not pierce, mark, or cut our bodies in any way, as tattoos permanently mark the skin.

The Bible gives multiple examples of heathens who cut their own bodies due to demon possession. First, the prophets of Baal cut themselves to no avail in the days of the prophet Elijah, thinking that their false gods would hear their requests.[309] Second, the maniac of Gadara, who was possessed with a legion of demons, cut himself with stones.[310] When a person willfully cuts or mutilates his or her own body, it is a clear sign of demonic activity and the individual must repent and seek deliverance through the power of the blood of Jesus Christ.

Christians who already have tattoos and feel the conviction of their mistake should first repent and vow never to get another marking on their body. Believers should not feel pressure to pay lots of money to remove their tattoos, though, as God is quick to forgive and ready to pardon confessed sins. Instead, the believer should try to cover up their tattoos, especially if the images or words are immoral.

---

309 1 Kings 18:24-29
310 Mark 5:2-5

HIGH HEELS

There are multiple reasons why high heels should not be worn by Christians and Jews. First, Scripture eludes to the haughty, prideful, and seductive daughters of Zion wearing high heel-like shoes in Isaiah 3:16: *"Moreover the Lord saith, Because the daughters of Zion are haughty, and walk with stretched forth necks and wanton eyes, walking and mincing as they go, and making a tinkling with their feet."* These judgment-bound women were mincing, or taking short steps. High heels naturally limit the length of each step. A tinkling noise as they walked sounds very similar to noise made when walking in high heels. Notice that their necks were also stretched out, which would be a result of wearing these unnatural footwear.

Second, scientific evidence supports both the damaging physical effects that wearing high heels have upon people and also sexual effects that high heels have upon the opposite sex. A research article from 2014 stated that high heels put excess stress upon the foot bones and ultimately damage the musculoskeletal system.[311] While preparing to write about high heels, I spoke with a licensed podiatrist about the effects of high heels. This doctor stated that high heels are the absolute worst shoe a human being could wear due to the damaging effects they have upon a person's entire body. He stated that during his training, multiple text books stated the fact that high heels never help the human body—they only damage it.

Christians are alarmed at any activity that damages their bodies, which are temples of the Holy Ghost. Believers do not belong to themselves but are the purchased property of Jesus Christ and therefore should not purposely prop up their bodies in a way that will lead to musculoskeletal damage later on in life.

Third, wearing high heels cannot be considered modest because they draw sexual attention to the wearer and lead others to harbor lustful thought of fornication or adultery. A 2017 study suggested that men are more attracted to women in high heels due to the lumbar curvature that high heels produce.[312] High heels must be the attire of harlots, as spoken in the Proverbs, since they

---

311 Ahmady, Amir, et al. "The Effect of Various Heights of High-heeled Shoes on Foot Arch Deformation: Finite Element Analysis." *National Center for Biotechnology Information*, www.ncbi.nlm.nih.gov

312 Al-Shawaf, Laith, et al. "Why Women Wear High Heels: Evolution, Lumbar Curvature, and Attractiveness." *National Center for Biotechnology Information*, www.ncbi.nlm.nih.gov

incite sexual lust.[313] Jesus said those with unconfessed lust, whether committed in the flesh or mind, will be guilty of adultery.[314]

Finally, recall that there is really nothing new under the sun.[315] High heels cannot be a new design in the twenty-first century that the world has never seen before. Rather, high heels are a revival of an older, rebellious, and seductive act.

CONCLUSION

Christian liberties allow believers to respectfully express their own preferences without being disobedient to God and without being under the condemnation of the devil. A great responsibility goes with this liberty, and Christians must consistently examine their choices to be sure they are influencing other believers in a way that builds their faith, rather than destroying it.

Wearing simple, inexpensive, and meaningful jewelry is a liberty for Christians. Jewelry worn in moderation will not cause genuine Christians to become prideful, but will serve as an expression of their faith or a sign of their marriage vows.

While jewelry has some Biblical support and offers some room for outward expression, makeup, tattoos, and high heels are vividly described as sinful acts in the Word of God and therefore should be avoided by all Christians. There is no liberty to sin in Christianity. Romans 6:1-2 states, *"What shall we say then? Shall we continue in sin, that grace may abound? God forbid. How shall we, that are dead to sin, live any longer therein?"*

---

313 Proverbs 7:10
314 Matthew 5:28
315 Ecclesiastes 1:9

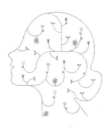

CHAPTER 6

Connecting the History of American Fashion and the Bible

"That thou keep this commandment without spot, unrebukeable, until the appearing of our Lord Jesus Christ:"

—*1 Timothy 6:14*

Connecting the history of American fashion to the Bible requires an in-depth study. This chapter is devoted to this essential endeavour. You'll learn when and why Americans forsook modesty. But first I will share a bit about my personal testimony and research into modesty.

JOYFUL RESEARCH

Researching for this chapter was an absolute labor of love for me and occurred over the course of the past two decades. When I first heard about the Bible's standards for a holy outward appearance in 2001, I was excited to be able to prove to my friends and family that all of these new teachings were Biblical and historically accurate. I wanted everyone to be enlightened by these new Bible truths as I had been. My enlightenment immediately transformed my own outward appearance, as my new love for Jesus was most easily expressed in how I could change my appearance to glorify Him. I was going to hold nothing back—I was willing to cut my long hair, start covering my thighs by wearing only long pants, and abstaining from taking off my shirt and showing off my chest. As I now reflect upon these changes, I can see that they were the natural outworking of the inward change that had already taken place in my heart through the cross of Christ.

For the first time in my life, as a new Christian and a college student, I found trips to the library exhilarating. My fiancée (now wife) and I spent hours digging through university libraries to search its books, encyclopedias, and almanacs in order to *"prove all things"* about a modest outward appearance.[316] Now I have a three ring binder filled with the findings as a witness that this nation once honored God's Word about modest clothing but has drastically backslidden.

My joy to research the truths of the Bible and connect them to American history came from a long desire I had to serve God. As a child, I knew God was real. In 1988, as a second grade student, God supernaturally healed my mother of cancer, without any radiation treatments, and she is alive today by the mercy of our Savior Jesus Christ. After her healing, my mother took all six of her children to different churches in the Toledo area testifying of God's healing power. At each church I heard again and again about the power of Jesus Christ. I always believed in God's power, but never experienced repentance for myself during that time.

In the next decade after my mother was healed, I grew into an adolescent passionate about sports rather than Christ. I selected friends that had the same selfish, sinful interests as I and I ran from God's call for my life. During this time, my mother would faithfully take all six of her children to church every Sunday and Wednesday. Many times I wanted to surrender to Jesus' call on my life, but I could not let go of the world's attractions. My change from a sinner to saint did not occur until I moved away from everyone I knew and attended the University of Akron.

I repented of my sins at an Athlete's in Action winter conference in December of 1999. About two years later, in the fall of 2001, I heard the truths about a modest outward appearance. I learned, in amazement, the guidelines for modest clothing and how tattoos, makeup, high heels, and other accessories were condemned by the Bible. I thought that if everyone could hear the truth I heard, they would quickly repent. Surely, all my female friends and family members would no longer cut their hair, wear makeup, nor wear pants, right?

---

316 1 Thessalonians 5:21

All my male friends would never get tattoos, nor wear immodest shorts, right? Boy, was I wrong!

Next came a separation time between my closest friends and I, as my Bible beliefs produced a new course of conduct in my life. It was painful, but essential. My best friend at the time wrote to me in an email that the devil was showing me the new doctrines I was believing. I felt heartbroken, but I could not deny the literal words of the Bible about each teaching.

This separation lead to a hunger to understand why the world was in its rebellious condition. Why wouldn't my friends, family, and country believe the plain, concise words in the Holy Bible? When and why did the masses turn from the holy ways of the Lord? The search for these answers became the driving motivation behind my library research. It seemed God led me to the right library books and even brought them into my education courses I was taking at the university. I felt as if God Himself was proving to me that His Bible standards were the absolute truth and all witnesses pointed to this fact.

THE HISTORY OF SEPARATE GARMENTS

Separate garments for men and women is usually the first noticeable difference between Christians and the world. My family has lots of first hand experience with looking different, as we have seven females, all in skirts, and two males, both in pants.

The first record of God requiring separate garments for men and women is found in the book of the law given to Moses, around 1400 B.C.[317] God told Moses that cross dressing was an abomination—a disgusting thing in His sight. Clothing provided order for gender, government, and culture. Without a separation of clothing, God knew that seeds of confusion would be planted into the fabric of society. These seeds of discrepancy would quickly grow into corruptible fruits, which is what we are seeing today through the transgender and LGBT movements. These groups have launched a complete assault on God's creative design and order for male and females established from the beginning of creation. Sadly, these modern Sodomites will only be stopped by the fire and brimstone of God's righteous wrath, just like the fate of Sodom

---

317 Deuteronomy 22:5

and Gomorrah. Believers must keep reaching out to them in hopes to save all who are ordained to eternal life.

Faithful, orthodox Jews have honored separate male and female garments from the days of Moses until today—nearly 3,400 years. This standard has stood the test of time, and even Jesus Christ Himself, Who never broke one command of God, never wore women's garments.

Christians also have honored the separation of male and female garments for nearly 2,000 years—from the days of the apostles until the present day. Just as God took cross dressing seriously, calling it an abomination, faithful Christians did the same. Greig and Smith (2003) noted that in 17th century England, a person of either sex could be hanged for dressing in the garments of the opposite sex.[318] As Christianity spread to North America, the laws of the land upheld this command, enforcing punishments like prison time and fines for those who cross dressed. Unfortunately, cross dressing became socially acceptable around the 1960s and 1970s. But faithful Christians have never stopped honoring Deuteronomy 22:5.

ANCIENT HEBREW CLOTHING

Since Deuteronomy 22:5 forbids cross dressing, what were the differences between the male and female garments? They were similar in one way but different in a number of ways. Their outer garments were similar in that they were both robes. That is where the similarities end, though, as the female robes were much longer with enough border and fringe to cover their feet.[319] The front of a woman's robe was long enough for her to tuck it up over her girdle to serve as an apron.[320] Male and female outer garments were also different in style[321] and could be easily differentiated at first glance, as men's garments resembled a coat-like cloak.[322] Although both sexes wore girdles, men's girdles

---

318 Greig, Cynthia and Catherine Smith. *Women in Pants: Manly Maidens, Cowgirls, and Other Renegades.* Harry N. Abrams, 2003
319 Packer
320 Packer
321 Breining, Heather. "Ancient Hebrew Clothing." *Ancient Hebrew Research Center*, www.ancient-hebrew.org
322 Matthew 5:40

were more prominent and important because they carried money and other necessities. Men's girdles also served to fasten their swords to their bodies.[323]

Based upon these differences, an individual's gender was instantly detectable at first glance to the onlooker. Female robes were much longer and male and female styles were noticeably different by God's holy design. Our Lord wants to keep reverential order among His people, with no gender confusion.

U.S. FASHION HISTORY BY CENTURY AND DECADE

I will now summarize and provide specific details about the fashion changes in the United States during the 19th and 20th centuries. Due to fewer societal changes, the 19th century is its own section separate from the 20th century. In the 20th century, each decade is described separately while highlighting the rapid increase of Scriptures that were being broken.

THE 19TH CENTURY

The majority of Americans kept the Bible commands for an outward appearance during the 19th century, but prostitutes and other small groups of women were guilty of breaking these commands. Prostitutes broke at least three of the four guidelines for modest clothing, as they exposed their body parts that God considered nakedness, wore skin-tight clothes, and cross dressed in men's clothing. These immoral ones were also part of the minority who wore makeup.

From mid-to-late century, small groups of women began wearing the pants-skirt bloomer costume, which broke the command of Deuteronomy 22:5. The invention of the bicycle and the freedoms it offered caused some women to cross dress with the excuses of comfort and function, but the move stalled out by the end of the century.

---

323 2 Samuel 20:8

SPECIFIC DETAILS

- Cross dressing was against the law and was punishable by arrest and imprisonment.[324]

- Women wearing pants in public was a deviant behavior.[325]

- "In the United States, the idea of women wearing pants of any kind caused an immediate and prolonged uproar."[326]

- It was very bad taste for a female to wear men's clothes or look masculine in any way.[327]

- Prostitutes were known for wearing tight, form-fitting pants and showed their bloomers or underwear to attract men. Society associated women in pants with prostitution. Prostitutes who worked in theaters revealed their flesh, especially their legs.[328]

- Amelia Bloomer helped explode a public controversy about dress reform when she suggested women wear men's trousers under a short skirt in the summer of 1851. The majority of people rejected this idea because of the Bible command in Deuteronomy 22:5, which was preached by the clergy.[329]

- "Bloomers did gain some converts in the 1850s, but the backlash was so strong that Amelia Bloomer and her colleagues gave up the fight."[330]

- Bloomers were associated with communal groups that believed in free love, i.e. adultery and fornication, and kept bloomers from being widely adopted.[331]

---

324 Greig and Smith
325 Beach, Stephen and Lindsey, Linda. *Sociology, 2nd Edition*. Prentice Hall, 2001
326 Macy, Sue. *Wheels of Change: How Women Rode the Bicycle to Freedom (With a Few Flat Tires Along the Way)*. National Geographic, 2011
327 Greig and Smith
328 Greig and Smith
329 Greig and Smith
330 Macy
331 Greig and Smith

- "[Amelia] Bloomer began to wear dresses made like other fashionable dresses, but with one shocking difference: the skirts were knee length. A proper woman did not reveal her legs, however. Even when swimming, women and girls covered up with long wool trousers beneath bathing dresses."[332]

- "The bicycle craze had a more lasting impact on women's clothing than just the use of bloomers."[333]

- "In the late 19th century, the bicycle impacted fashion, causing women to abandon frilly skirts and corsets in favor of sensible bloomers."[334]

- The women's education move of the 1870s permitted female students to cross dress during performances but most did not allow men to attend those shows.[335]

- "With makeup frowned upon, women drank vinegar and ate chalk to achieve a pale complexion."[336]

- "Women continued [19th century] to wear their hair long and pulled back from the face, usually piled atop the head."[337]

THE 20TH CENTURY

During the first half of the 20th century, the majority of Americans honored God's standards for modest clothing and a holy outward appearance. The Roaring 20s was the exception, as millions of women, for the first time, cut their hair, wore makeup, and exposed parts of their bodies that their parents and grandparents would not have dreamed of exposing. These rebellious ones, called flappers, joined sinful men and smoked, drank, danced, and arrogantly defied the following Scriptures: 2 Kings 9:30, Jeremiah 4:30, Ezekiel 23:40, 1 Corinthians 3:17, 11:1-16, Galatians 5:21, 1 Thessalonians 5:7, 1 Timothy

---

332 Miller, Brandon Marie. *Dressed for the Occasion: What Americans Wore 1620-1970.* Minneapolis: Lerner Publications, 1999
333 Macy
334 Macy
335 Greig and Smith
336 Miller
337 Miller

2:9, and 1 John 2:15. The Great Depression caused a financial crisis that sent most Americans back to a humble way of life, including fashion choices throughout the 1940s and 1950s.

The second half of the 20th century saw the majority of Americans completely reject a Biblical, modest outward appearance. The Sexual Revolution emphasized free love, unisex dressing and hair styles, and led to the full acceptance of cross dressing in the 1970s. The backsliding trend was unstoppable through the 1980s and 1990s, as nearly every body part came into full view on America's streets and beaches. Americans abandoned even more Scripture, including Deuteronomy 22:5, Proverbs 7:10, Romans 1:26-27, 1 Thessalonians 4:3, and Revelation 3:17.

THE 1910s

During World War I, many women wore pants while working in factories and experienced financial independence while the men were away fighting in the war. After the war, most women went back to wearing dresses and their previous lifestyles, but seeds of change had been planted. Skirt lengths shortened.

SPECIFIC DETAILS

- Women would not be caught dead wearing pants in public at the time of the first World War.[338]

- "By 1915, skirts had shortened to the ankle."[339]

- "The United States entered World War I, 1914-1918, in June 1917. For the first time, women joined the American armed services. Civilian women performed a wide variety of wartime jobs. Most worked in ankle-length dresses. Some, especially in factories and on farms, opted to wear trousers. Fashion for women again appeared in turmoil. Should women abandon pants and return to prewar styles? Wearing the 'pants in the

---

338 L'Amour, Louis. *The Outlaws of Mesquite*. Random House Publishing Group, 1990
339 Miller

family' meant being in charge. With husbands and fathers back home, women in pants returned to dresses. But change was in the air."[340]

THE 1920s

The Roaring 20s was the first time in American history in which millions of women publicly transgressed God's commands for a modest outward appearance. For the first time, women cut their hair, wore makeup, and adopted seductive and luxurious fashions. The only force that could and did slow down this immoral trend was the Great Depression, which God seemingly allowed to humble the nation.

SPECIFIC DETAILS

- Women bobbed their hair and the hemlines of their skirts raised to the knee. Some women wore trousers in public, blurring the gender lines, in order to both express lesbian desires and their equality with men.[341]

- "In August 1920, after decades of lost battles, American women won the right to vote through the 19th amendment to the U.S. Constitution. Women's new freedom at the ballot box soon mirrored a new freedom in clothes."[342]

- "Short hair and simple hats brought freedom from the anxiety of keeping a huge or elaborate hat pinned to an equally elaborate hairstyle. Women cut their hair and everybody said, 'How practical!' The woman instinctively realized that here was a passport to freedom in daily life which she was not going to let go. The convenience of short hair has been appreciated by many women ever since the bob, the shingle, and Eton crop of the 20s."[343]

- Rouse noted that changes were not all liberating, but some actually became a form of slavery, such as wearing makeup. She wrote, "It was now [1929] commonplace for women to wear makeup. In the Victorian

---

340 Miller
341 Greig and Smith
342 Miller
343 Rouse, Elizabeth. *Understanding Fashion*. Grafton Books, 1989

period it had been considered immoral to 'paint' one's face and many older people still subscribed to this view. But now women could be seen everywhere pouting at their compact mirror in an attempt to achieve the desired cupid's bow with the aid of lipstick and dabbing at their noses with a powder puff. The advent of Hollywood and its stars had made the open use of cosmetics acceptable but it also brought a new bondage for women, that of trying to look like someone else."[344]

- "The new decade [Roaring 20s] transformed young women's fashion as never before. For the first time, women grabbed their long hair, which had always been so time-consuming to style, and snipped it off. 'Bobbed' hair was all the rage. The boyish bob was chin length or even shorter. A sleek cut that swung close to the face, the bob called for a hat that also hugged the head."[345]

- "The flapper painted on lipstick and rogue produced by companies run by women such as Helen Rubinstein and Elizabeth Arden. Although women hid their curves in the tubular silhouette [dresses with no waistline], they revealed more skin. All through the decade, skirts inched higher and higher. Some states considered fines for dresses shorter than three inches above the ankle. But the trend was irreversible; by 1926, women's dresses rose, for the first time, above the knee. Bathing costumes shrank to sleeveless tank suits."[346]

- "By the 1920s, skirts for women were short."[347]

- "For not only were women's clothes changing—many women now had short hair and wore makeup."[348]

- "After World War I ended, big changes were afoot. Not only had women won the right to vote, but dancer Irene Castle had bobbed her hair. As the 20s roared in, more and more women headed for beauty shops to have their hair bobbed. At the time, few women were eager to have their 'bobs' done in a barbershop with a row of men watching and snickering.

---

344 Rouse
345 Miller
346 Miller
347 "Dress." *New Britannica Encyclopedia*, 1992
348 Rouse

In many cases, this would be the biggest decision the woman would ever make—to cut off a lifetime growth of hair, knowing her husband, father or boyfriend was dead set against it. In our town, this new style [shingle cut] seemed to usher in the Flapper Age. Next came short skirts, rolled-down hose, discarded corsets and cigarette smoking. It was like a revolution!"[349]

- In 1922, a Washington D.C. beach had officials check the bathers' swimsuits to be sure they were no more than six inches above the knee.[350]

- Chicago police arrested women wearing revealing bathing suits for indecent exposure in 1922.[351]

THE 1930s

In the 1930s, the Great Depression affected most Americans, causing some to return to their humble lifestyles and modest expressions of fashion. While God was drawing His little flock back to Himself, Satan used this economic downturn to lure millions into inexpensive movie theatres. Hollywood's evil influence multiplied during this era, especially in the area of makeup. Women came into a new bondage of imitating the facial cosmetics of female movie stars. Women followed Hollywood rather than God's Word, breaking the command to imitate God: *"Be ye therefore followers* (imitators) *of God, as dear children."*[352]

There were a few famous women renegades who dared to defy the Bible commands for modest clothing, but their impact had little effect on the majority of Americans. Most women continued to wear long skirts and dresses.

SPECIFIC DETAILS

- Katharine Hepburn and Marlene Dietrich were some of the first women to wear men's pants publicly in the 1930s and 1940s.[353]

349 Williamson, Ethel. "Short Hair, Long Career." *Reminisce Magazine.* January/February 1997
350 Time-Life. *The Roaring 20s: The Decade That Changed America.* 2017
351 Time-Life
352 Ephesians 5:1
353 Greig and Smith

- Marlene Dietrich made international headlines in 1933 when she appeared offscreen in men's clothing. The Paris chief of police threatened to make her leave town if she continued to wear pants so Dietrich changed into a skirt but still wore a man's collar, tie, and hat.[354]

- "To ease the sting of economic burdens, Americans looked to Hollywood. More than 85 million people a week escaped their troubles in darkened movie theaters. Many fans imitated the polished makeup of film stars: plucked eyebrows, dark lipstick, gleaming fingernails."[355]

- "As much as possible, women also emulated the clothing of the movie queens. Men also copied their idols. Clark Gable took off his shirt in one movie and revealed that he had no undershirt beneath. Since not wearing an undershirt was a fashion anyone could immediately afford, undershirt sales plummeted. Hollywood popularized an image of fitness; it became fashionable to show off a well-toned body. For swimming, men abandoned tank suits that covered their chests, and for the first time, appeared at beaches bare-chested. Some women tossed out their long tennis dresses and copied tennis champ Alice Marble, who in 1933 dared to wear shorts to Wimbledon. Hollywood also promoted the tan. For centuries women had prized a pale complexion as a symbol of leisure. People who got tan worked outdoors doing manual labor."[356]

THE 1940s AND 1950s

By the 1940s and 1950s, most Americans were still dressing modestly but skirt lengths for women kept rising inch by inch. Famous female actresses continued to cross dress in men's pants. Other rebels were wearing two piece bathing suits, but those outlandish fashions were not the norm—yet.

---

354 Rubinstein, Ruth. *Dress Codes: Meanings and Messages in American Culture*. Westview Press, 1995
355 Miller
356 Miller

SPECIFIC DETAILS

- "Shocking! The most shocking new style of all was the two piece bathing suit, which used less fabric than the more modest one piece suit popular before the war."[357]

- "High school style: [1949-1959] Although uniforms were not required at American schools, teen girls developed their own—the skirt, either full or pencil shaped finishing just below the knee, and sweater or fitted top. Pants and jeans were forbidden."[358]

- The styles of the 1950s provided a physical barrier between the sexes, which was the same approach as the Victorian era. The styles made it seem the clothes were not easily removed.[359]

- Audrey Hepburn wore Capri pants in the 1950s.[360]

THE 1960s

The Sexual Revolution of the 1960s literally changed everything in fashion for the majority of Americans. In this decade, the godly standards for outward appearance began to fall drastically. Miniskirts rose far above the knee for the first time, exposing more flesh than ever. Little clothing was being worn and the material was light. Fashions focused on sexual availability.

By the end of the decade, two major trends defied God's law about cross dressing. First, unisex fashions created a sense of confusion amongst the youth. Second, Levi's created it's division for women's pants in 1968, making pants readily available to women for the first time ever.

It is noteworthy that in the early 1960s the Supreme Court removed prayer and Bible reading from public schools. The results of removing Jesus Christ and His standards for modest clothing from schools has been decreased academic achievement, increased crime, drug use, and sexual immorality.

---

357 Gourley, Catherine. *Welcome to Molly's World, 1944: Growing up in World War Two America.* American Girl Publishing, 1999
358 Dorling Kindersley. *Smithsonian Fashion: The Definitive History of Costume and Style.* DK Publishing eBooks, 2012
359 Rouse
360 Greig and Smith

SPECIFIC DETAILS

- Clothing styles suggested accessibility and sexual availability.[361]
- Prominent zips and fastenings made it seem clothing was easily removed. Lighter clothing and much less clothing became popular.[362]
- Pant suits became increasingly popular during the 1960s and 1970s.[363]
- Skirt length was the most important fashion consideration for the majority of Americans.[364]
- Unisex dressing was a new trend in part due to the hippy movement. Women wore men's jeans and shirts in the 1960s. Some men grew their hair out like women and were suspended from school or lost their jobs.[365]
- "In real life, the biggest trend in women's fashion was the miniskirt. Introduced in London boutiques by designer Mary Quant and others, the mini had a hemline eight or nine inches above the knee, exposing more skin than any previous skirt. 'The young recognize no boundaries and feel no commitments,' proclaimed a New York Times Magazine article. 'Short skirts, some say, are a sign.' But how were women supposed to sit or bend without exposing more than they wished? Patterned tights and the first panty hose resolved that problem, but not another."[366]
- "The hippies' dress reflected their break with society [carefree lifestyles, including drug use, sexual promiscuity]. Both sexes wore jeans, sandals, and flowing caftans. Young males grew their hair to shoulder length. Older folks complained that they couldn't tell the boys from the girls. 'Men's clothes have become an approximation of women's, and women's clothes copy men's,' one psychologist noted. 'When clothes express such confused roles—society is in big trouble.' "[367]

361 Rouse
362 Rouse
363 Greig and Smith
364 Murray, Maggie Pexton. *Changing Styles in Fashion: Who, What, Why.* Fairchild Books, 1989
365 Rouse
366 Miller
367 Miller

- "British designer Mary Quant was the first to introduce dresses above the knee in 1960."[368]

- "Women gooped their eyes with black eyeliner and colored eye shadow."[369]

- "The short skirts and low waists of the 1920s were again fashionable in the 1960s. London's 'Mod' look from Carnaby Street of the 1960s lead to an erratic era of fluctuating hemlines and unisex fashions."[370]

- "But if women's hair was getting shorter, some men were wearing their hair longer; hairstyles for some young people became almost identical."[371]

- "Stemming from the unisex fashions by futuristic designers such as Pierre Cardin and André Courrèges, fashionable women began wearing pants in the 1960s and 70s. The sexual revolution and 'women's lib' meant that women were taking greater strides to enter the workforce, and as a result they borrowed more from men's fashion. French designer Yves Saint Laurent (YSL) first created his sleek but controversial Le Smoking tuxedo suit for women in 1966, and continued to create androgynous styles each season. The look slowly became more widely accepted as an alternative to skirts and dresses."[372]

THE 1970s

The main fashion theme of the 1970s was women wearing pants. During the early part of the decade, companies and fine restaurants would not allow women to wear pants in their establishments, but their standards eventually weakened and cross dressing became a part of everyday life. Public teachers unions played a big role in allowing women teachers to begin wearing pants to school. Women in pants hit prime time television as well, as Mary Tyler Moore was the first woman to wear pants on a television sitcom.

---

368 *Collier's Encyclopedia*, 1995
369 Miller
370 "Dress." *New Britannica Encyclopedia*, 1992
371 Rouse
372 Dorling Kindersley

SPECIFIC DETAILS

- One word can sum up women's fashion in the 70s—pants. Women wearing pants was their solution to the problem of previous decades about how long dresses and skirts should be. Most fine restaurants in the early 1970s would not allow women to enter if they were dressed in pants.[373]

- Public school teacher unions helped women gain the right to wear pants to school in the early 1970s, as long as the material and color matched the top.[374]

- Trouser outfits were finally accepted as everyday wear but not in the majority. Women in pants solved the hemline controversy. Unisex clothes were advertised in London and discussion arose about the psychological implications that would result.[375]

- In the early 1970s, it was common to see men and women dressed identically, in unisex fashion, with the same hair styles. It was more common to see women borrowing from male fashion, especially among feminists.[376]

- "As the 1970s opened, many women, burned out on skirts by the mini, began to wear pants. Pants sold so well that major designers added pant suits—including some for elegant evening wear—to their collections. In 1968, Levi's launched a 'division for gals.' Some businesses began to accept female employees in pants. One survey reported that Macy's department store would not permit women employees in pants, but the First National Bank of Boston would 'if they continued to act like women.' AT&T would keep 'an open mind.' For the first time in America's fashion history, women began to have a real choice between dresses and pants. Mistress Fuller, or any woman of the 1600s or 1700s, never would have dreamed of pulling on a pair of breeches."[377]

---

373 Murray
374 Kopkowski, Cynthia. "Then and Now." *NEA Today Magazine*, September 2006
375 "Fashion and Dress." *Britannica Book of the Year*. Chicago: William Benton, 1970
376 Rouse
377 Miller

- Mary Tyler Moore was the first woman to wear pants on a television sitcom in the 1970s. The writers of her show limited her to one scene per show in which she could wear pants.[378]

- The no-bra look became popular in the early 70s.[379]

THE 1980s AND 1990s

The 1980s and 1990s produced even more disobedience to God's standards for modest clothing. Major fashion statements were spread through the punk, hip-hop, grunge, and goth movements.

The trends of cross dressing and exposing more flesh were irreversible. The most shocking of all fashion statements was in swimwear. String bikinis and thongs revealed nearly every part of the human body. Satan had propagated and achieved a condition of complete nakedness and undress.

SPECIFIC DETAILS

- The length of the skirts and dresses of women was no longer a major issue by the late 1980s.[380]

- Fashion trends were made popular through the punk, hip-hop, grunge, and goth movements.[381]

- On the beaches of America, "even more radical expressions like thongs revealed breasts and buttocks."[382]

---

378 "Mary Tyler Moore was the First Woman Ever on a Sitcom to Wear Pants." *Teen Vogue*, www.teenvogue.com
379 Rouse
380 Murray
381 Dorling Kindersley
382 Pollard, Jeff. *Christian Modesty and the Public Undressing of America*. San Antonio: The Vision Forum, Inc. 2004

REAPING THE WHIRLWIND

The United States of America is in the same position that Israel found itself in during the days of the prophet Hosea—awaiting the judgment and wrath of Almighty God. Hosea warned northern Israel of the pending judgments upon them for their breaking of God's covenant and their transgressions of His laws around 750 B.C. The United States has done the same through the legalization of sin and the breaking of nearly every law of God, including God's standards for a modest and holy outward appearance.

Hosea stated the following words about Israel's rebellion against God—Israel had *"sown the wind"* and would *"reap the whirlwind."*[383] The phrase *"sowing the wind"* is a proverb from the agricultural practice of sowing and reaping, or planting and harvesting. Sowing and reaping is a law of God. Whatever we plant in our lives, we will harvest the consequences, whether good or evil, as Galatians 6:6-7 teaches: *"Be not deceived; God is not mocked: for whatsoever a man soweth, that shall he also reap. For he that soweth to his flesh shall of the flesh reap corruption; but he that soweth to the Spirit shall of the Spirit reap life everlasting."*

Israel had planted seeds of rebellion and disobedience against the commands of God and they were sure to multiply into an awful, deadly harvest of the judgments of God. The whirlwind came in 722 B.C. when the Assyrian armies invaded the capital city of Samaria and carried the people of Israel away into captivity.

The United States has also *"sown the wind."* Remember that America upheld God's modesty standards for the outward appearance for a few hundred years. But America has fallen from its love for God. The historical facts from this chapter show that evil seeds of disobedience have been planted through the Roaring 20s, the Sexual Revolution of the 60s, the cross dressing move of the 70s, and the state of undress of the 80s and 90s.

America is beginning to see a whirlwind develop in cities, families, governments, businesses, and communities all over this country. It is the whirlwind of sexual abuse, homosexuality, and the transgender lifestyle. The small seeds of undressing women, cross dressing, and unisex fashions of the 1960s and 1970s that were planted into millions of minds have now matured into corruptible fruit—a cultural majority that hates the truth of God's Word and is worthy of

383 Hosea 8:7

the judgments of God. The United States, along with many other countries, is reviving the evil condition of Sodom and Gomorrah, fulfilling Jesus' prophecy.[384]

The whirlwind of sexual abuse is howling in both Hollywood and in churches. The "Me Too" movement of 2018 has exposed Hollywood's wicked glorification of sexuality, unveiling its' rotten, toxic, filthy, and God-hating atmosphere. Scores of female celebrities have come forward to accuse and bring conviction upon rich and powerful sexual predators like Harvey Weinstein and Bill Cosby.[385] Churches have experienced this violent wind, as an August 2018 Pennsylvania grand jury report found that Catholic priests had sexually abused over 1,000 victims in the past 70 years.[386] These allegations join a growing list of sex abuse cases spanning the globe, from Louisiana to Ireland, and from the Netherlands to Australia.[387]

The cross dressing and unisex fashions of the 1960s and 1970s were the seeds of confusion that led to the current rise and widespread adoption of homosexuality and transgenderism. God is not the author confusion.[388] If you plant or allow confusion, or any seed of sin, the harvest will be only death.[389]

In the sight of God, those who accept homosexuality and the transgender movement are insane. Paul said that homosexuals have received a reprobate mind and are without natural affection.[390] In the Greek Lexicon, the reprobate mind is a "worthless, rejected, castaway"[391] mindset that God gives to those who will not retain and accept the knowledge of God. A person with a reprobate mind cannot be in his or her right mind, making them insane in the sight of God. Furthermore, the person is without the natural affection that God intended men and women to have. The natural feelings of human beings to be attracted to the opposite sex have eroded. The natural feeling to remain the gender of your birth has also been abandoned by millions in this backslidden country.

Paul taught that a reprobate mind actually hates the Word of God. This

---

384 Luke 17:28-32
385 "MeToo: A Timeline of Events." *Chicago Tribune*, www.chicagotribune.com
386 "Catholic Priests Abused 1,000 Children in Pennsylvania, Report Says." *The New York Times*, www.nytimes.com
387 "Timeline: A Look at the Catholic Church's Sex Abuse Scandals." *CNN*, www.cnn.com
388 1 Corinthians 14:33
389 James 1:15
390 Romans 1:18-32
391 *Voice of God Recordings Inc.*, "The Bible: Hebrew and Greek Lexicons," www.branham.org/en/messagesearch

God-hating condition is the result of people refusing to worship God and be thankful for His revealed truth.[392] The apostle also wrote that the wrath of God, or whirlwind, would come upon the entire world for this evil. We know this judgment includes the United States because the majority of its citizens have chosen sin over righteousness and *"all nations"* have been deceived by the antichrist spirit.[393]

Retain the knowledge of God in your mind. Worship the Creator and not the creation. Love the truth of God's Word. Sow to the Holy Spirit and reap eternal life. Receive the truths God is currently restoring to His children.

CONCLUSION

The history of fashion in the United States reveals the immoral, sinful downfall through a public undressing of its men and women. Lucifer, like a serpent, has slowly slithered through the decades, destroying God's holiness standards and establishing his own cultural garden—Satan's Eden. America, like Israel, was once a God-honoring nation but has transgressed the commands of the Bible and will soon reap the full whirlwind of the judgments of God.

Through my research, I realized that most people do not have any idea about the standards of holiness that our nation used to keep. The same thing happened to Israel after Joshua's generation passed away. A generation rose up that did not know the Lord. *"And also all that generation were gathered unto their fathers: and there arose another generation after them, which knew not the Lord, nor yet the works which he had done for Israel."*[394]

Hardly anyone knows that most women never wore makeup or cut their hair until the 1920s because of their fear of Almighty God. Few Americans know that it was a public disgrace for most females to wear pants to school and work until the 1960s and 1970s because the masses heard preaching about Deuteronomy 22:5.

Recognize the purpose that God's Spirit has been revealing these truths to you, as 1 Corinthians 2:12 says *"Now we have received, not the spirit of the world, but the spirit which is of God; that we might know the things that are freely given*

---

392 Romans 1:18-32
393 Revelation 18:23
394 Judges 2:10

to us of God." Before the wrath of God falls upon America, it is your job, and my job, to spread the truth of God's Word to everyone that will listen. Share God's truth about modest clothing with a lost and dying generation. Share God's truths with your words in conversation. With your modest clothes. With your social media account. With your daily life.

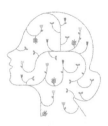

CHAPTER 7

YouTube Testimonies, Questions and Answers

"But sanctify the Lord God in your hearts: and be ready always to give an answer to every man that asketh you a reason of the hope that is in you with meekness and fear."

—1 Peter 3:15

YouTube, the video sharing company owned by Google, is one of the most popular websites on the internet. It is astounding that over one billion hours of video are watched daily on YouTube.[395] Nearly two billion users access this site—which is over a third of all the people on the internet.

Christians should use YouTube as a platform to spread the gospel of Jesus Christ. Through videos Christians can provide humble, direct answers to the questions people have about Jesus Christ and the Bible.

Believers should also avoid all sinful content on YouTube. David wrote by the Holy Spirit that *"I will set no wicked thing before mine eyes: I hate the work of them that turn aside; it shall not cleave to me."*[396] A Spirit-filled and Spirit-led Christian will not purposely place evil content before his eyes, but rather cast down any video that exalts itself against the Word of God.[397]

---

395 "YouTube For Press." *YouTube*, www.youtube.com/yt/about/press.
396 Psalm 101:3
397 2 Corinthians 10:5

MY DESIRE FOR OUTREACH

Although I did not publish my first YouTube video until October 2014, there had been a burning desire in my heart to create and distribute Christ-glorifying content since 2004. During the ten years leading up to 2014, I dreamed of spreading the truth of God to anyone who would listen. It was such a burden that in 2005 I asked my pastor if we could hold special Saturday night services in order to record sermons that would teach people about the Bible. He agreed and we recorded two audio sermons about the dangers of television and the two seeds (wheat and tares). One friend of mine burned these audio files onto CDs and we distributed the sermons to friends and strangers. I was immediately hooked on outreach!

In 2006, I became pastor of the church I currently pastor in Akron, Ohio. One of our first ministries was copying and distributing audio sermons and teachings. The ministry lasted for a few years and then stopped, as our family sizes increased and caused us to focus more on establishing godliness in our growing families. The burden to share the gospel continued though, and as 2014 approached, I began slowly tinkering with video editing, filming, and script writing. I could not escape the deep call I was hearing to go beyond audio and create my own teaching videos to spread the gospel of my Savior, Jesus Christ.

In March of 2014, after many hours of preparation, I finally had enough courage to publish my first video on Vimeo, titled "Water Baptism By Scripture Alone." I chose Vimeo because I felt it was a safer platform at the time. After uploading eight more teaching videos, I was surprised to see that I had not received any online abuse and decided I should move to a more widely-used website—YouTube. I am so thankful for the results I have witnessed since joining YouTube.

With over 500,000 views and 6,000 subscribers to my YouTube page, I rejoice in the hand of God to spread His truth via the internet. God has provided numerous testimonies that have resulted from the 50-plus YouTube Bible-teaching videos I have uploaded. I want you to know how the revelations about God's standards for a modest outward appearance have helped change lives around the world, reaching countries I could have never stepped foot onto. My prayer is that these testimonies will help inspire you to experience the life-changing power of Jesus Christ's Word for yourself in every area of your life—including your outward appearance. Each of us need a testimony of our own experience with our Lord Jesus Christ in order to overcome Satan! *"And they overcame him by the blood of the Lamb, and by the word of their testimony; and they loved not their lives unto the death."*[398]

TESTIMONIES

Most Christians find testimonies to be an extremely powerful source of encouragement. Our faith is uplifted, challenged, and raised after hearing how God has helped another believer. Jesus Christ's real presence is more powerfully felt when believers share how God faithfully and personally answered their pleas.

I have extracted the following testimonies from my YouTube channel and email account that related to a modest outward appearance. The first two testimonies, though, are not about the outward appearance, but I felt you would benefit from hearing how the truths of God's Word make believers speechless and save lost souls.

GENERAL COMMENT ABOUT ALL THE VIDEOS

"Your videos play a huge role in my life. I've got no words to say. I've become speechless about your help. I think I better say I love you, my pastor." —N.S., November 2016

COMMENT ABOUT THE WATER BAPTISM VIDEO

"Your YouTube channel not only helped me to know God better but also guided me to follow God's will. Hopefully, [the videos] will save and help a lot more lost souls like me. Thanks to you for making those videos! You saved my soul." —D.P., November 2017

---

398 Revelation 12:11

MAKEUP VIDEO TESTIMONIES

"I fasted three days and asked God to show me about makeup and I just opened my YouTube and here you are talking about makeup. It was amazing! God answered my prayer! Many thanks, brother. You really helped me. I will share this video with other sisters." —L.H., September 2017

"Thank you for this video. It made me realize there is no such thing as 'modest' makeup and there are churches twisting verses of the Bible to keep their members." —K.A., January 2018

"I'm not wearing makeup no [sic] more." —T.J., January 2018

"I'm throwing away my makeup." —G.M., October 2017

"Thank you for this video. I don't wear a lot of makeup but I'm completely done with what I was using." —L.S., October 2017

"The argument you made, based entirely on God's holy and perfect word, has convinced me." —H.L., August 2017

"I need to share with you what has happened with me since I commented on this video. As I said, I was a makeup guru. I loved how I could transform and look like someone else. But God! One morning shortly after I wrote to you, God said, 'Why not skip the makeup this morning and spend that extra time with me?' I obeyed and loved it. Little by little, makeup became less and less attractive. Sometimes it wouldn't even go on right and I would have to wash it all off! Everyday I noticed how in the evening, as it was wearing off, my face looked worse than it did without any makeup on. Then one day I was reading Scripture and the thought came to me and said 'Why do you paint your face to gain man's approval?' So I thought and that was why I did wear it. I loved the attention I got and the compliments every week about how pretty I was. I stopped wearing makeup cold turkey after that. Yes, I felt naked and self conscious at first. I have now gone about two months without it and I don't miss it most days. I don't feel naked without it either. I don't get near the compliments from men or women as I used to, but that's okay because that could lead me down a wrong path anyways." —G.M., July 2017

LONG DRESSES FOR WOMEN VIDEO TESTIMONIES

"I have been struggling for many years regarding my wardrobe. I have read the Scriptures and listened to opinions expressed by Christians throughout these years regarding this subject. I have searched the internet seeking for answers. Finally, I picked up my phone yesterday and I came across Pastor Jesse Smith's message regarding Long Dresses and the Bible. After listening to this message I cleaned out my closet completely. I would like to thank you for clarifying the importance of dressing modestly. I am really grateful to God and to this ministry, for today I can say I no longer wish to dress as I did, but according to the Bible." —M.C., January 23, 2016

Two days later, M.C. wrote more:

"She [a friend from church] was extremely happy that I shared this video with her. Once again, I am very grateful to God and yourself [sic] for the impact this video has had in my life. I was able to visit our neighborhood Goodwill and purchased some skirts and dresses at a very reasonable price. I shared this testimony with a family member and she offered to purchase some additional skirts/dresses for me from the Goodwill on Friday. Praise God! God never fails!" —M. C., January 25, 2016

"I watched this video many months ago and your message left a seed inside of my soul. I have been wearing skirts and dresses for the last few months and I feel liberated. I cannot go back to wearing pants because the Holy Ghost makes me feel dirty. Thank you for putting this profound message on the internet." —K.A., January 2018

"I truly wanted to thank you for the video on women dressing modestly and how unscriptural it is for females to be wearing pants. You presented the message quite well and it was educational and enlightening. In the last few weeks the Lord has laid it on my heart to totally dress in modest apparel (long skirts/dresses) and to ditch all the pants and shorts. What a shame that very few churches take a stand on modesty. You are to be commended for speaking the truth in love. It seems that 99.9% of American women wear pants and don't give it a second thought. It was a blessing watching your teachings on that subject. I appreciate the work you put into it. Again, thank you!" —L.F., October 2016

HAIR LENGTH VIDEO

"Thank you, Brother Smith. This was a blessing to me and I fully understand now that I should not even trim my hair." —G.L., June 9, 2016

"Thank God for this message. Before, I used to cut my hair like a boy but I will never in my life cut my hair again. Now I know it is against God's Word. Thank you so much, man of God." —P.F., August 2017

MODEST CLOTHING VIDEO

"I have just watched your video on YouTube concerning what Christians should wear and what the Bible teaches about nakedness. I just wanted to say what a good video it is. I am tired of Christians making excuses for exposing legs and other parts of themselves and trying to use the Bible to justify it. I was very glad to find your video which explains it in such a clear way." —M.D., July 7, 2016

"I watched the videos on your YouTube channel about modest clothing. Immediately I was aware that I needed to make adjustments on the clothing that I currently own. I am so blessed to have come across your channel, by the way." —G.N., May 28, 2017

"Thank you for delivering your message in a kind, loving way. It's confirmation. I actually asked God, 'How do you want me to dress?' Then I stumbled upon your video. Glory to God." —M.S., November 2017

"Thank you, dear. I'm transformed." —J.C., September 2017

FREQUENTLY ASKED QUESTIONS

Answering viewers' questions on my YouTube channel has been one of the most challenging and rewarding experiences. It is very challenging at times because I am limited in my knowledge and experience. Despite the uneasy feeling at the pit of my stomach when I read a question I have never heard before, the uncertainty drives me to dig deeper in the Word and history in order to find the truth. As a result, the reward is learning more about God's Word, which I am then able to preach to my congregation. I love how this process challenges me to be more like the Bereans, who searched the Scriptures daily in order to know the truth.[399]

Each topic below—makeup, long dresses, and hair length—will include three or more questions and answers. I tried to choose the most frequently asked and most challenging questions. At times the punctuation and grammar were edited for clarity.

MAKEUP QUESTIONS

Question 1: "God bless your heart for trying to correct the Body of Christ, but the Scriptures you cited spoke to the 'heart' of evil Jezebel and the rebellion of Israel. What about Esther who took an entire year to prepare for the king?" —P.S., January 2018

Answer: "Dear friend, Thank you for the respectful tone of your comment. First, the three Scriptures I quoted [on the YouTube video] clearly identified face painting as an evil trait, as God never asked anyone to face paint, and all three women were under the judgment of God for their idolatry. Second, Esther never painted her face. There seems to be a huge misunderstanding among churches with Esther, as she never used facial cosmetics. She was purified using oils, but not face painting. Esther cannot be used as an example to support makeup wearing, as she was never given cosmetics. Esther 2:9 and 2:12 state that she was given *'things for purification'* which were *'oils of myrrh'* and *'sweet odors.'* It never says she was given makeup to paint her face."

Question 2: "What about a lady who has defects, like acne or scars, from an accident or surgery? What about a bad burn that can be covered with full cover foundation? A little blush. C'mon? What about if it's your daughter or your wife with aging spots feeling ugly in front of you?" —R.C., November 2017

Answer: "Thank you for the questions. First, I am very happy you refrain from lipstick and other makeup. Second, I would encourage those with scars to seek God about this topic, but since we know God never changes, so it would seem

---

[399] Acts 17:11

God would give them the same answer—makeup is a heathen trait that should be avoided. When people see their scars, the women could use them for a testimony about the grace of God for keeping them healthy or alive. Third, we teach women and men should never wear any makeup, under any condition. I know that seems harsh to you, but we obey based upon our love for Jesus and His Holy Bible. You said a 'little blush' is acceptable, but to me, I respectfully say that your words remind me of a 'little leaven' leavens the whole lump (1 Corinthians 5:6). A little bit of sin is still sin and will grow into more sin. A little bit of worldliness is still worldly. We must not love the world, neither the things that are in the world. Last, if my wife or daughters feel ugly due to aging spots, I will reassure them that I love them unconditionally and that they are fearfully and wonderfully made in God's sight and mine."

Question 3: "God tells us to obey His commandments, so obviously those are sins. Is wearing makeup and trousers sinful? They're obviously 'out of order,' as God is an orderly God, but are they truly sins? Or is it semantics? Just curious." —B. J., November 2017

Answer: "Thank you for the question. Cross dressing, or men wearing skirts and women wearing pants, is a sin and even more, an abomination (Deuteronomy 22:5). Makeup is a sin as well, as God told Israel not to learn the ways of the heathen (Jeremiah 10:2). Makeup wearing is an expression of pride. Also, a proud look (what could be more prideful than wearing a false face to impress others?) is an abomination (Proverbs 6:16-17)."

LONG DRESSES FOR WOMEN QUESTIONS

Question 1: "Pastor Jesse Smith, if you have answered this before, excuse me, I don't have the strength to read all of the comments below. This rule [no cross dressing] was made back in the times when men wore robes, Jesus included. Men and women wore what we would call 'skirts' now. The women wore head coverings, and men covered their heads when they were praying or traveling in the heat. So when did this rule pertain to 'pants,' if originally men and women both wore robes with belts tied around the waist?" —P.L., December 2017

Answer: "Yes, the rule of Deuteronomy 22:5 was made around 1300 B.C.

Faithful Jews have observed separate garments for men and women ever since. Orthodox Jewish women wear long skirts to this day. Jesus never sinned according to Hebrews 4:15, so we know even He kept the rule of Deuteronomy 22:5. The robes in the days of Jesus had multiple layers, such as when Jesus spoke of coats and cloaks (Matthew 5:40). But the robes had to have been different for men and women, for God commanded a difference in garments. From what I have read, the women's garments were longer than the men's and dragged against the ground. Plus, the outer robes were styled differently, so an observer could tell instantly if the person was a male or female at first glance. Throughout all history, since the days of Moses, all believers, whether Jew or Christian, have had a separation of garments for men and women. As for pants, men began to wear them in the 1600s and have worn them ever since. Women did not start wearing pants regularly until the 1970s. In our Judeo-Christian culture, the founders of the faith chose pants for men and dresses for women—and God honored them by making the United States the greatest and most prosperous nation in the history of the world. I believe God did this because the founders loved Christ, the Bible, and holiness. Now the United States has fallen from God. But in each culture, they have the responsibility from God to wear separate garments since the Bible does not literally say 'pants' and 'dresses.' Recently, Bruce Jenner's decision to cross dress opened the eyes of true Bible believers to the need for men to dress like men and women to dress like women. He is committing an abomination by dressing like a woman. This same outcry about his immorality was the same outcry in the 20th century when women began wearing pants. Read 'Women in Pants' by Cynthia Greig and Catherine Smith."

Question 2: "So if we are going to be consistent in using the Deuteronomy 22:5 passage, should we not follow the same teaching with all of these other items of clothing—pants, t-shirts, socks, underwear, skirts, and blouses?" —D.H., December 2016

Answer: "First, I would say that if you question the validity of the pants on women, you need to study deeper into the subject. I hope you will devote some time into searching for the truth, for if you do, you will find it. God promised to reveal truth to those who would seek for it. Second, as for every item of clothing, I cannot say that we must make every item separate, for the Bible does not teach that, as far as I know. But on a personal level, yes, my wife and I do not wear any of the same clothes. She does not wear my shirts. We have separate socks and all other garments. She looks like a woman and her outer garments reveal her female gender. I look like a man and my outer garments reveal my masculine gender. Lastly, think of the social disgust when Bruce Jenner came out as a 'woman' in 2015. One reason this was so evil was because he was breaking Deuteronomy 22:5—dressing as a woman—which is an abomination. The public disgust that many expressed at Jenner's cross dressing was the same disgust that society expressed when women began wearing pants in the 1940s through 60s. It is historical and factual. Let me know if you want the resources."

Question 3: "Why can't pants be modest? What about women that work out? It can be rather dangerous to work out in long skirts. I do agree with modesty. I just don't see why it has to be long skirts all the time. I can be perfectly modest and covered in pants. Plus, most jobs that young girls can get (entry level) will require you to wear slacks." —B.B., February 2016

Answer: "Thank you for the comment. First, pants on a woman can technically be modest—loose (not tight) and covering the loins, thighs and lower legs—but yet there still must be a separation in men's and women's garments according to Deuteronomy 22:5, so we do not believe women should ever wear pants. Technically, a dress on a man could be modest, but the fact the man would be wearing garments pertaining to a woman would break the Word of God and be wrong. Second, I know numerous women who work out in full length skirts. It is only dangerous if a person participates in dangerous exercises. I think the wisdom of God would tell our hearts to not endanger our bodies and avoid exercises that are dangerous. Surely you can find alternative exercises that are less dangerous and get the same results. Third, it has to be long skirts for women all the time because God said so. Jesus kept all the law and never sinned. He honored all the Old Testament, including Deuteronomy 22:5, all the time. Jesus wore garments that pertained to men all the time. We should follow His example, wouldn't you agree? Fourth, if a job required a woman to wear men's clothes, she should look elsewhere for a job in order to honor God's Word. Any job that required a believer to disobey the commands of God would not be in the plan of God for their life, I believe. If we honor God, God will honor us and provide a job for us, as He is Jehovah-Jireh, our provider."

HAIR LENGTH QUESTIONS

Question 1: "How about if the ends of the hair are split, frazzled, and damaged? Is just trimming those ends to encourage a woman's hair to grow even longer and healthier an exception?" —C.M., August 2017

Answer: "Friend, we do not find any trimming of women's hair in the entire Bible—from cover to cover, from Genesis to Revelation. At our church, we teach that a woman is not instructed to cut, trim, or shave any hair from her head because we never see God instructing godly, obedient women to do so in the Bible. Also, there are some differing opinions that trimming keeps hair healthy. I have heard from numerous Christian women who never trim their hair that say their hair is healthier because they do not trim the split ends. Hair must be taken care of and cared for daily so as not to encourage breaks. Having a healthy diet and lifestyle will also limit the amount of split ends. At our church, we simply teach the Bible, which never gives any godly woman the command to cut or trim her hair in any way."

Question 2: "How long do you think a man's hair is allowed to be? What would you say is the maximum length?" —C.B., December 2017

Answer: "That's a good question, sir. I would say the longest hair length for a man would be to the neck or shoulder area, but that is just my own idea. Recall that Jewish priests were to have short hair, and Paul commanded Christian men to have short hair (Ezekiel 44:20, 1 Corinthians 11:14). As men, we always want to make sure we are the leaders in holiness and modesty. Men's hair must show that there is a separation between male and female. This is why I recommend that the men in our church cut their hair quite short so that their male gender is instantly perceived by those that look at them."

Question 3: "Umm, didn't Jesus have shoulder length hair?" —E.M., November 2017

Answer: "We do not know the exact length of Jesus' hair, but again, even shoulder length hair on a man is not uncut hair. Uncut hair is what God commands for all women in 1 Corinthians 11:1-16. Women are called to not cut their hair—ever. Men are called, in the New Testament, to cut their hair. If you cut your hair, you are obeying the Bible. Since you are a man, you should seek to keep your hair short, for a woman's hair should be uncut. If you grow your hair long and do not cut it, you are disobeying the Bible. God wants women to have uncut hair, so the shorter hair that men have, the more different they will look than women. God wants a separation and difference between men and women in their hair, duties in life, and even outer garments. Many images of Christ show Him with shoulder-length hair, but that length would be much shorter than the women of His day, who probably had uncut hair down to their waists, if not longer."

Question 4: "Is God unfair because I do not have long hair? I'm an African American woman." —M.C., August 2017

Answer: "Friend, God is not unfair. I am sorry if there is a misunderstanding about my video. I apologize that my video did not address the issue of how some women of different races cannot grow long hair. God wants all women to have uncut hair, no matter the race. The actual length does not matter. God wants women to have uncut hair. God never asked a godly woman to cut her hair in the entire Bible. As long as a woman's hair is uncut, we know God's Word is kept and fulfilled. God is pleased with women as long as they do not cut their hair. God is not asking for 12 inches of length, 24, or any other specific number of inches. He is only asking for uncut hair."

THE MOST FREQUENTLY ASKED QUESTION

After answering hundreds of questions on YouTube and via email, there has been one question that has been asked more than any other in regards to a modest outward appearance. The question has been asked in various ways, but at its core can be stated as the following: "Since the Bible says that God looks on the heart and not the outward appearance, why should I care about my outward appearance?" The question is suggesting that 1 Samuel 16:7 teaches Christians should not worry about the outward appearance, but this is certainly a misapplication of Scripture, which states *"But the LORD said unto Samuel, Look not on his countenance, or on the height of his stature; because I have refused him: for the LORD seeth not as man seeth; for man looketh on the outward appearance, but the LORD looketh on the heart."*[400]

At first glance, this question might seem to have some validity, but the wisdom of the Holy Spirit gives us at least three reasons why 1 Samuel 16:7 does not excuse Christians from having standards for their outward appearance.

First, this question has taken 1 Samuel 16:7 out of context and applied it in a way that God did not intend. In context, 1 Samuel 16:7 is God's correction to His prophet, Samuel, about how He chooses a king. Samuel was in Bethlehem at Jesse's to anoint the next king of Israel to replace Saul, the rebellious king. Samuel had seen some of Jesse's sons and assumed that Eliab, Jesse's oldest son, would be the Lord's anointed, or future king, based upon his physical stature. But the faithful God corrected Samuel by letting him know that He did not choose kings based upon their countenance or height. God revealed that He chose kings based upon the condition of their hearts and David was a man after the heart of God.[401] The context of 1 Samuel 16:7 is not about makeup, hair length, separate garments for men and women, or modest clothing. A Bible teacher, anointed of the Holy Spirit, would rightly divide 1 Samuel 16:7 and place it in its proper context, which is God's requirements when choosing a righteous king. Applying 1 Samuel 16:7 to say that God is not interested in our outward appearance would be a complete misapplication.

Second, 1 Samuel 16:7 cannot disannul or negate the numerous commands of God elsewhere in Scripture about out outward appearance. Remember 1 Timothy 2:9? Paul commanded women to wear modest clothing. He lived around 1,000 years after Samuel and still commanded Christian women to wear modest clothing. There is no record of Paul writing that Christians do not need to care about their outward appearance since God cared only about their hearts. Remember 1 Corinthians 11:1-16? Paul taught that it is a shame for a man to have uncut hair and for a woman to have trimmed hair. I could keep reminding you of all the Scriptures from previous chapters in this book that command believers to conform their outward appearance to God's loving preferences but I will stop here because I trust that the Holy Spirit has shown you the error of using 1 Samuel 16:7 to give people a license to present themselves with a worldly, sinful outward appearance.

Third, the outward appearance often—not always—reveals the condition of

---

400 1 Samuel 16:7
401 Acts 13:22

the heart, and the Bible is full of examples. Cain, the murdering son of the wicked one, changed his facial countenance after God rejected his disobedient sacrifice and eventually left the presence of God in full rebellion to the Word of the Lord.[402] Saul's countenance changed for the worse when the evil spirits were troubling his mind.[403] Evil, whorish women used seductive facial expressions in order to tempt men into acts of adultery and fornication.[404] The clothing of harlots revealed their occupation.[405] The maniac of Gadara was naked because of the influence of the legion of demons inside of him.[406] Based upon these five examples, it would be foolish to say God does not care about the outward appearance.

Of course, the outward appearance does not always reveal the true condition of the heart, as the Pharisees proved during the earthly ministry of the Lord Jesus Christ. Jesus said that these evil, wicked, hypocritical children of hell had a clean, beautiful outward appearance but were full of dead men's bones.[407] This truth is evident today, as many of the world's major religions require that their leaders and followers dress modestly and yet their idolatry, hatred, and rejection of the gospel of Jesus Christ proves that they, too, are the children of hell—the spiritual children of their father, the devil.[408]

Undoubtedly, God cares much about the outward appearances of His children, as I have demonstrated through the scores of Scripture cited in this book's previous chapters. God does indeed look upon our heart condition but our obedience to or rejection of the rightly divided Word of God reveals our heart condition to those around us. Let us obey the Bible's doctrines about our outward appearance from the heart: *"But God be thanked, that ye were the servants of sin, but ye have obeyed from the heart that form of doctrine which was delivered you."*[409]

---

402 Genesis 4:5, 6, 14, 1 John 3:12
403 1 Samuel 16:14-23
404 Proverbs 6:24-26
405 Proverbs 7:10
406 Luke 8:35
407 Matthew 23:15, 25-28
408 John 8:43-45
409 Romans 6:17

CONCLUSION

God is still spreading His Word through many channels, one of which is YouTube. Just as the printing press of the 19th century drastically increased spreading the truth of God's Word, today the internet does the same. Along with the spread of truth, though, comes questions, which the vigilant Christian will be prepared to answer.[410]

The Holy Bible has all the answers we need for the questions people have about the way of holiness. If we search the Scriptures as Jesus commanded, as the Bereans modeled, we will find the life-giving answers to all inquiries about the ways of God.[411] This is why regular church attendance is absolutely necessary for a genuine Christian. Paul taught that the five preaching gifts in the house of God would answer all our questions, bringing believers to completion and stability in the faith.[412] David, the man after the heart or will of God, had this same respect for the house of God. David knew God's faithfulness in revealing His will to His people in the house of God. He knew God would reveal His will through the teaching of His Word in His house, saying *"One thing have I desired of the LORD, that will I seek after; that I may dwell in the house of the LORD all the days of my life, to behold the beauty of the LORD, and to enquire in his temple."*[413]

We know God does the same today as we gather in our churches and feast upon the preaching of truth.

While I am thankful for the internet helping to spread the gospel, I know it is a secondary tool of God. The Lord's primary tool is live preaching with the anointing and power of the Holy Ghost, as Jesus commanded in the Great Commission.[414] The disciples obeyed this command, preaching the gospel, and the Lord worked with them, giving them supernatural signs.[415] Our church will continue to do the same and experience the same results, by God's grace.

---

410 1 Peter 3:15
411 John 5:39, Acts 17:11
412 Ephesians 4:11-14
413 Psalm 27:4
414 Matthew 28:18-20
415 Mark 16:20

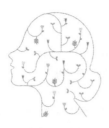

CHAPTER 8

The Perfect Will of God

> *"I beseech you therefore, brethren, by the mercies of God, that ye present your bodies a living sacrifice, holy, acceptable unto God, which is your reasonable service. And be not conformed to this world: but be ye transformed by the renewing of your mind, that ye may prove what is that good, and acceptable, and perfect, will of God."*
>
> —*Romans 12:1-2*

At Paul's conversion, his trembling, astonished being asked the Lord Jesus Christ this humble question, *"Lord, what wilt thou have me to do?"*[416] The gracious God answered him and told him to go into the city of Damascus and he would be told more about what he must do. Every true, sincere-hearted Christian will ask the Lord the same thing today—"What must I do?" In other words, "What is your will for my life, Lord? What do you want me to do?"

In the case of this book, I hope you've asked yourself this question: "Lord, what is your will for my outward appearance?" Hopefully you have been asking this question for years. If you sincerely asked this question as a prayer, God will give you His perfect will according to His Holy Bible.

PROVING THE PERFECT WILL OF GOD

Romans 12:2 teaches that Christians can not only know the will of God, but prove what is the perfect will of God for their lives. This is what children of

---

[416] Acts 9:6

the light do. We walk in the light, or will of God, and prove *"what is acceptable unto the Lord."*[417] In fact, every part of our lives should be proven to be pleasing to God, Paul taught.[418] Once we know God's perfect will, we must abide in it.

What will be your evidence or proof of the will of God? It will be the actions that are acceptable to God based upon the Scriptures the Holy Spirit anointed godly men to write for our admonition. There is no other proof or evidence we need than the Word of God, for Jesus Christ said the Word of God *"is truth."*[419]

In order to prove the perfect will of God, Paul wrote that we needed a transformed mind. The Greek word for "transformed" in Romans 12:2 is the same word used to describe the "transfigured" presence of Jesus Christ on the mountain in Matthew 17:1-8.[420] Jesus' transfiguration included a face that shined like the sun, and raiment bright as light. Paul said this is what should happen to our minds when we know the perfect will of God—our minds are illuminated as the sun! The *"Day Star"* has risen in our thoughts and mind![421] Darkness, confusion, and fear have all vanished. The truth of God is present in our thoughts and shining in all its glory. There is no confusion about what God wants done in our lives when we know the perfect will of God through a transformed mind. To the believer, the truth of the Word of God becomes a "Thus saith the Lord"—an unquestioned, authoritative love request from his Savior, the Lord Jesus Christ.

Today, as in every generation, Satan will battle Christians and try to move them out of walking in the perfect will of God. Those who reject the will of God and accept a sin-loving lifestyle are called workers of iniquity, proving that there is no sin or disobedience in the perfect will of God.[422]

TWO PATHS: PERFECT VERSUS PERMISSIVE

There are two paths we can walk—either the perfect will of God, or the permissive will of God. The perfect will of God is the way of full obedience to the Word of God while the permissive will of God is the path or way of

---

417 Ephesians 5:10
418 1 Thessalonians 5:21
419 John 17:17
420 *Voice of God Recordings Inc.*, "The Bible: Hebrew and Greek Lexicons," www.branham.org/en/messagesearch
421 2 Peter 1:19
422 Matthew 7:21-23

disobedience and compromise. The Word of God is the light unto our path, as David wrote.[423] If we lose our light, or Scriptural guidance, we will walk in a permissive path rather than the perfect path and reap the consequences of disobeying the Lord.

Scripture gives us numerous examples of individuals who chose to walk in the permissive will of God rather than the perfect will of God. The following four examples—Cain, Balaam, Saul, and Hezekiah—prove there is great danger in choosing the permissive will of God, but a person can still be saved despite walking away from the perfect will of God. Ultimately, God is the Righteous Judge and will grant eternal life to all those He has foreknown.

Cain was given the perfect will of God—animal sacrifice—by God Himself. This took place after Cain witnessed his brother Abel offer an animal sacrifice which pleased God. The animal sacrifice was received by God as the perfect will of God.[424] Instead of humbling himself and obeying the perfect will of God, Cain spurned the mercy of God, changed his countenance, murdered his brother, and left the presence of God. This proves God will accept nothing but true worship, the perfect will of God, according to His revealed will, which is what Jesus Christ taught as well.[425] It seems likely that Cain was lost.[426]

Balaam was a genuine prophet, foretelling the Star of Jacob that would lead the wise men to Christ.[427] But Balaam rejected God's perfect will, which was against his joining forces with king Balak. After Balaam heard God's perfect will, telling him not to go see Balak, he prayed again to see if God would tell him different.[428] Balaam did not need a second word from God because he was already given the perfect will of God. Because Balaam's soul loved money more than God's perfect will, he chose the *"wages of unrighteousness"*[429] and prayed to see if God would let him go with the men. God saw Balaam's wickedness and let Balaam have His permissive will. Once teamed up with Balak, Balaam preached false doctrine and caused Israel to commit acts of fornication that led to the death of thousands of people.[430] Peter taught that Balaam's destiny was

423 Psalm 119:105
424 Genesis 4:3-8
425 John 4:23-24
426 1 John 3:12
427 Numbers 24:17
428 Numbers 22:15-21
429 2 Peter 2:15
430 Numbers 25:9, Revelation 2:14

hell, *"the mist of darkness forever."*[431] Balaam stands as an example of a gifted individual, who could hear from God, but loved money more than righteousness. He ultimately rejected salvation.

Israel's first king, Saul, is an example of someone being saved despite choosing the permissive will of God for the majority of his adult life. We know Saul was saved because the spirit of Samuel, called up out of paradise by the witch of Endor, told Saul that he would be with him in paradise the next day.[432] But Saul's life will be remembered for walking in the permissive will of God, as Saul's pride and hatred caused him to rebel against the perfect will of God. His sins caused him to lose out on God's establishing his kingdom *"forever."*[433] What tremendous rewards Saul lost because he chose the permissive will of God! And guess who Saul lost his kingdom and reward to? David, the man who was after the heart of God, or the perfect will of God! Saul had a premature death, as God Himself took his life because of his awful transgressions of God's Word.[434]

King Hezekiah's life was one of honor and obedience to the God of Israel for the majority of his life. At the end of his life, though, Hezekiah choose to walk in the permissive will of God. His first mistake was to ask God for more years to his life after the prophet Isaiah had told him to set his house in order, in preparation for his death. Scripture says it would have been better for Hezekiah to die rather than live the extra 15 years because after his healing he catered to the Babylonian ambassadors and showed them all of the treasures in the Lord's house.[435] Hezekiah remains a striking example of a postmature death, as he died at a later time than God had desired because he chose the permissive will of God.

Now I will return to today. A Holy-Ghost filled Christian will have the same desire as Christ—to walk in the perfect will of God. Did you know that it was Jesus' delight to obey the Word of God? We must have this same mindset as Christ, that it is a joy to do the will of God as revealed in the Bible. David wrote the following of Christ:

---

431 2 Peter 2:17
432 1 Samuel 28:19
433 1 Samuel 13:13-14
434 1 Chronicles 10:13-14
435 2 Kings 20:1-6, 2 Chronicles 32:24-31

> *"Then said I, Lo, I come: in the volume of the book it is written of me, I delight to do thy will, O my God: yea, thy law is within my heart."*[436]

When you are born again, the commandments of God are not grievous. Obeying the Word is not difficult when you are sealed with the baptism of the Holy Ghost in your being, for you contain the quickening power of the risen Christ in your soul! *"By this we know that we love the children of God, when we love God, and keep his commandments. For this is the love of God, that we keep his commandments: and his commandments are not grievous. For whatsoever is born of God overcometh the world: and this is the victory that overcometh the world, even our faith."*[437] Paul says, *"But if the Spirit of him that raised up Jesus from the dead dwell in you, he that raised up Christ from the dead shall also quicken your mortal bodies by his Spirit that dwelleth in you."*[438]

If you want to do the perfect will of God, you must have a teachable heart, as David wrote: *"Teach me to do thy will; for thou art my God: thy spirit is good; lead me into the land of uprightness."*[439] Jesus then explained how humble and sincere you must be if you want to learn from Him, saying *"Come unto me, all ye that labour and are heavy laden, and I will give you rest. Take my yoke upon you, and learn of me; for I am meek and lowly in heart: and ye shall find rest unto your souls. For my yoke is easy, and my burden is light."*[440]

You must come with a humble heart to learn from Jesus Christ. You cannot come to Christ, and His Bible, with a prideful heart saying, "I can dress however I want and still go to heaven. I don't have to submit to what the Bible teaches about makeup, my hair length, or modest clothing." If you want to learn from the Meek One, Himself, the Lord Jesus Christ, you must become meek like Him. Meekly, prayerfully, pick up your Bible and let God's Word prove the perfect will of God for your outward appearance.

---

[436] Psalm 40:7
[437] 1 John 5:2-4
[438] Romans 8:11
[439] Psalm 143:10
[440] Matthew 11:28-30

PROVING THE PERFECT WILL OF GOD FOR YOUR OUTWARD APPEARANCE

Through the previous chapters, you have been reading the perfect will of God for your outward appearance because the teachings were completely Bible-based. A brief review will help assure you that this is God's proven, perfect will.

Beginning with modest clothing, recall the Scriptures taught in Chapter 3. The Bible teaches we must cover all areas of nakedness, which include the area from our shoulders down to past our knees according to the following Scriptures: Genesis 3:21, Isaiah 47:1-3, Revelation 1:13, 1 Kings 18:46, Proverbs 31:17, and Matthew 5:40. These Scriptures prove that the perfect will of God is to cover our bodies from our shoulders to our shins by God's design—not mine. If we wear clothes that reveal any body parts within this range, we have broken the perfect will of God and are living in the permissive will of God. Exposing shoulders, bearing the navel, exposing cleavage, and exposing thighs are acts included in the permissive will of God. Can anyone prove this teaching wrong, according to the Bible? I humbly offer the challenge to be proven wrong by the Word of God. I can find no Scriptural witnesses of God being pleased when people present their uncovered shoulders, cleavage, navel, and thighs.

Are shoulder-exposing tank tops, halter or tube tops, and spaghetti-strap shirts the perfect will of God? No, those shirts expose the shoulders. Shoulders are nakedness in the sight of God, for they are part of the breast and arms region. Can anyone prove this wrong by the Bible?

Are mini-skirts, sundresses, high-slit skirts, low-cut dresses, short-shorts and shorts, on men or women, the perfect will of God? No, as all of these garments expose the thigh area, which God considers nakedness according to Isaiah 47:1-3. Can anyone prove this wrong by the Bible?

Modest clothing must also include multiple layers or be thick and opaque according to Genesis 3:21, Matthew 5:40, Judges 3:16, and John 21:7. Peter, in John 21:7, was wearing only his undergarment-tunic and was considered naked in the sight of God. Like Peter, anyone who wears their undergarments on the outside, such as underwear or bathing suits, is guilty of walking in the permissive will of God. Can anyone prove this wrong by the Bible?

Are bikinis and skin-tight one piece bathing suits the perfect will of God? No, these suits are one thin layer of clothing and are equal to the amount of fabric used for undergarments. They also reveal breasts, the navel, thighs, and all the leg. Bathing suits reveal nearly every area of nakedness. Can anyone prove this wrong by the Bible?

Are sheer blouses the perfect will of God? No, for these shirts allow men to see through the outer garments and perceive undergarments. God calls the exposing of undergarments nakedness. Can anyone prove this wrong by the Bible?

Modest clothing must be gender-specific according to Deuteronomy 22:5, as even the Lord Jesus obeyed this command of separate garments for men and women. In our American culture, any man who wears women's clothing—dresses, bras, etcetera—is committing an abomination. Likewise, any woman who wears pants is cross dressing and walking in the permissive will of God. Can anyone prove this wrong by the Bible?

Modest clothing must also be loose according to 1 Kings 19:13, Mark 16:5, Revelation 6:11, 7:14, and Proverbs 7:10. Anyone who wears skin-tight clothing, thus revealing the form of their bodies, is walking in the permissive will of God. Can anyone prove this wrong by the Bible?

Are skinny jeans, yoga pants, and women's leggings the perfect will of God? No, for they reveal the literal shape of the human body, which is a form of nakedness that can cause others to lust after their bodies and commit spiritual fornications and adulteries. Can anyone prove this wrong by the Bible?

Concerning our outward appearance, recall the Scriptures taught in Chapters 4, 5, and 6. We can prove the perfect will of God for our hair length, jewelry, and skin.

Men's hair length must be short and women's must be as long as possible, as women must never cut their hair.[441] Any man who lets his hair grow uncut is bringing shame upon himself. Likewise, a woman who cuts or trims her hair in anyway is bringing herself shame, along with her head, her husband. Can anyone prove this wrong by the Bible?

Are uncut dreadlocks on a man the perfect will of God? No, for men are commanded to have short hair. Can anyone prove this wrong by the Bible?

Are bobbed hair cuts or the trimming of split ends the perfect will of God for women? No, for godly women are never commanded to cut their hair in any way. Can anyone prove this wrong by the Bible?

---

441 1 Corinthians 11:1-16

Jewelry can be worn in moderation, with a meek and quiet attitude, as long as the jewelry is not extremely costly.[442] Wearing jewelry such as rings, bracelets, and necklaces in this manner can be the perfect will of God. Can anyone prove this wrong by the Bible?

Jewelry that is extremely expensive is in the permissive will of God.[443] So is wearing any jewelry, whether inexpensive or expensive, with a prideful heart. Wearing large amounts of jewelry is also the permissive will of God.[444] Can anyone prove this wrong by the Bible?

Makeup, tattoos, and high heels are not part of the perfect will of God according to the following Scriptures: 2 Kings 9:30, Jeremiah 4:30, Ezekiel 23:40, Leviticus 19:28, and Isaiah 3:16. Can anyone prove this wrong by the Bible?

If all these statements cannot be proved wrong by the Bible, then these statements must be the perfect will of God for our outward appearance.

I am not guessing what is the perfect will of God concerning our outward appearances. By the grace of God, I have shown you much more than *"two or three witnesses,"* as Jesus and Paul required, to prove that these teachings are correct. As Jesus said, I say humbly concerning these guidelines for a modest outward appearance, *"Which of you convinceth me of sin?"*[445] Which Scripture have I failed to teach properly? Who am I causing to stumble with these Bible guidelines on modest clothing and outward appearance? I am pointing you to present your body to God as a living sacrifice.

ASK FOR AND SEEK REVELATION

Perhaps you want a transformed mind in order to do the perfect will of God, but you still may feel like you do not understand all the Scripture I have presented thus far. If the Bible feels like a newspaper, like a dead letter, then it is time you ask and seek God for revelation. Revelation is an unveiling of God and His will. Revelation is more important to you than you know, for the Lord Jesus Christ said that the gates of hell cannot prevail against revelation: *"And Jesus answered and said unto him, Blessed art thou, Simon Barjona: for flesh and*

---

442 1 Timothy 2:9, 1 Peter 3:3
443 1 Timothy 2:9
444 Isaiah 3:16-24
445 John 8:46

blood hath not revealed it unto thee, but my Father which is in heaven. And I say also unto thee, That thou art Peter, and upon this rock I will build my church; and the gates of hell shall not prevail against it."[446]

In context, Jesus was declaring to Peter how blessed he was that God, not man, had revealed to him that Jesus was the Messiah, or Christ. The revelation, or unveiling, of who Jesus was would be the anchor that would keep Peter grounded in God's love. Satan would try to overthrow Peter's faith,[447] but the revelation Peter received from Father God would prevail over all of Satan's counsel to destroy him.

The same is true about revelation for all of God's teachings. You need revelation about a modest outward appearance, forgiveness, gifts, and love. You name the topic, and you need revelation about it. All revelation from God will empower His children to serve Him and overcome the devil. Revelation was so crucial that Paul prayed for believers to receive it:

> "*Wherefore I also, after I heard of your faith in the Lord Jesus, and love unto all the saints, Cease not to give thanks for you, making mention of you in my prayers; That the God of our Lord Jesus Christ, the Father of glory, may give unto you the spirit of wisdom and revelation in the knowledge of him: The eyes of your understanding being enlightened; that ye may know what is the hope of his calling, and what the riches of the glory of his inheritance in the saints, And what is the exceeding greatness of his power to us-ward who believe, according to the working of his mighty power.*"[448]

The power and importance of revelation was so great that even our Lord Jesus rejoiced over His disciples receiving His revelations: "*In that hour Jesus rejoiced in spirit, and said, I thank thee, O Father, Lord of heaven and earth, that thou hast hid these things from the wise and prudent, and hast revealed them unto babes: even so, Father; for so it seemed good in thy sight. All things are delivered to me of my Father: and no man knoweth who the Son is, but the Father; and who the Father is, but the Son, and he to whom the Son will reveal him.*"[449]

---

446 Matthew 16:17-18
447 Luke 22:31-32
448 Ephesians 1:15-19
449 Luke 10:21-22

If you are struggling to understand the Scriptures I have pointed out, then I encourage you to continue seeking God's will for your outward appearance. With all your heart, ask, seek, and knock for revelation, as Jesus promised everyone that did this would receive of Him: *"Ask, and it shall be given you; seek, and ye shall find; knock, and it shall be opened unto you: For every one that asketh receiveth; and he that seeketh findeth; and to him that knocketh it shall be opened."*[450]

There is one very important passage about seeking God's will that has been pivotal in many of my times of seeking the will of God for my own life. After you read Proverbs 2:3-9 below, I hope you will be unashamed and confident when crying out to God for the revelation of His Word!

> *"Yea, if thou criest after knowledge, and liftest up thy voice for understanding; If thou seekest her as silver, and searchest for her as for hid treasures; Then shalt thou understand the fear of the LORD, and find the knowledge of God. For the LORD giveth wisdom: out of his mouth cometh knowledge and understanding. He layeth up sound wisdom for the righteous: he is a buckler to them that walk uprightly. He keepeth the paths of judgment, and preserveth the way of his saints. Then shalt thou understand righteousness, and judgment, and equity; yea, every good path."*[451]

THE SOURCE OF MY TEACHINGS

After reading these nearly 40,000 words contained in eight chapters, you may be wondering who is the source of my teachings. To begin with, I humbly state that I have no teachings of my own. With the help of God, I teach only the doctrine of our Lord and Savior Jesus Christ. He is the ultimate, divine source of my teachings, for it is His Bible that I have used to rightly divide these truths about a modest outward appearance.

But you are probably still wondering which human source, meaning which man or ministry, did I follow in order to gain these doctrines. I am happy

---

450 Matthew 7:7-8
451 Proverbs 2:3-9

to share that I received these Bible doctrines from the ministry of the late Reverend William Branham (1909-1965).

William Branham's ministry is the human source of my teachings, yet God was the divine source. God revealed His Bible truths to Branham, as the Word of the Lord always comes to the prophet.[452] The prophetic Spirit of Elijah anointed William Branham, fulfilling Jesus' promise in Matthew 17:11 to "*restore all things*"—including Christian modesty.

In November of 2001, I was introduced to the ministry of "Brother Branham," as we lovingly call him, and have followed his Bible-based teachings ever since.

The simplest way to describe the ministry of Brother Branham is by calling him a prophet of God. A New Testament prophet is an official preaching office of God according to Ephesians 4:11. The qualifications of a prophet include hearing from God,[453] foretelling the future in the name the Lord without fail,[454] and revealing secrets that were previously hidden.[455] By the leading of the Holy Spirit, Brother Branham met these three qualifications.

Brother Branham heard from God throughout his entire life, meeting the requirement of Numbers 12:6. He shared many of his supernatural encounters with both the Lord Jesus and the Angel of the Lord. During his entire ministry, the Angel of the Lord followed him, just as Moses and Paul had an angel with them during their lives.[456] In 1946, the Angel of the Lord visited Brother Branham and commissioned him to pray for the sick with a gift of divine healing. After hearing from and obeying the Angel of the Lord, the healing campaigns of Brother Branham were miraculous, to say the least, and led to a spiritual explosion in the Pentecostal movement of the 1940s, 1950s, and 1960s.[457] Brother Branham's ministry spearheaded this world-wide movement.

A true prophet foretells future events without fail, as Moses taught in Deuteronomy 18:20-22. Brother Branham met this prophetic requirement. My YouTube video titled "Three Prophecies of William Branham" details three prophecies that have either come to pass already or are in the process of coming

---

452 2 Samuel 24:11, Jeremiah 37:6
453 Numbers 12:6
454 Deuteronomy 18:20-22
455 Amos 3:7
456 Exodus 23:20-23, Acts 27:23
457 Burgess, Gary, et al. *Dictionary of Pentecostal and Charismatic Movements*. Grand Rapids: Zondervan, 1998

to pass, which include the immoral condition of the churches in the United States, no greater ministry rising to the Gentile people than what God gave to Brother Branham, and no return of Christian denominations to an apostolic ministry. Along with these three prophecies, there are many other future prophecies that I believe will come to pass as detailed in my YouTube video "Thus Saith the Lord—Future Prophecies of William Branham."

Because God is so gracious, He has always sent a prophet to warn His people before times of judgment, as seen in four clear examples. First, in the years before the flood of judgment in Noah's day, the merciful God sent at least two prophets to warn the people—Enoch and Noah.[458] Second, before Israel's Babylonian and Assyrian captivity, God sent multiple prophets to warn the people, such as Jeremiah, Isaiah, Micah, and Habakkuk. Third, God sent the prophet Jonah to warn the Ninevites before judgment, and thankfully they repented and were spared from the wrath of God.[459] Fourth, God sent the prophet John the Baptist and His Son, Jesus, to warn Israel before the destruction of Jerusalem at the coming of Titus in 70 A.D.[460] Finally, at the end of the world, the unchanging God was obligated to send a prophetic ministry to warn the people before the next judgment, which will be the great tribulation period of the wrath of God, spoken of in Daniel 12:1, Revelation 6:12-17, 11:18, 15:1, and 16:1 to name a few. The ministry of Brother Branham was God's prophetic voice of warning, but also of deliverance!

One of the most exciting elements of a prophetic ministry is that prophets revealed God's secrets that were previously hidden according to Amos 3:7: *"Surely the Lord GOD will do nothing, but he revealeth his secret unto his servants the prophets."* God revealed many secrets to Brother Branham, which he in turn revealed to us, including, but not limited to:

- the human identities of the seven stars, or angel-messengers to the seven churches in Revelation 1:20 and chapters 2 and 3

- the revelation of the Seven Seals of Revelation chapters 6 and 8

- the 12 New Testament mysteries

- the restoration of the one faith of the apostolic fathers

---

458 Genesis 6:13, Jude 1:14
459 Matthew 12:39
460 Matthew 3:7, Luke 7:28, 23:28-31, Acts 3:22

- the visitation of the Son of Man (Jesus Christ) to the Gentiles before world-wide judgment

- the last sign to the Gentiles before world-wide judgment

- the identity of the final two Gentile kingdoms—Greek and Roman—that followed the first two kingdoms (Babylon and the Medes and Persians) described in Nebuchadnezzar's dream in Daniel chapter 2

- the United States' identity and position in Revelation 13

- the mark of the beast, his number, and image

If you seek to learn more about the amazing, prophetic ministry of Brother William Branham, please contact me through our church's website at www.brideofchristohio.org. Please do not neglect the God-ordained, supernatural ministry of Brother Branham. According to the Holy Spirit, speaking prophetically through Brother Branham in 1961, his supernatural ministry was the "last sign to the Gentile church before the rapture. Thus saith the Word of God. Thus saith the Holy Spirit."

I am so thankful that I did not neglect this ministry, and I will end this section by sharing how this ministry has impacted my life.

The ministry of Brother William Branham has established a true relationship between the Lord Jesus and myself. While I am thankful for the charismatic church I was raised in, it did not contain the pure, unadulterated Bible teachings that God gave to His servant, Brother Branham. While on my own during my college years, I attended many different churches, but their preaching could not produce victory in my life, as I was still a slave-addict to many sins, and felt extremely helpless. But shortly after I heard the Bible-based revelations God gave to Brother Branham, the presence of Jesus Christ became a reality to me and I was completely delivered of my sinful addictions. Not long after my deliverance, I began to see the power of God move even more in my own life and preaching ministry. One highlight was an evangelistic trip to Guyana in 2011, where I saw God cast out devils in the exact same manner as the Lord Jesus modeled in Mark 9:25-27. God so anointed and filled my body that I saw myself rebuking foul spirits, who would cry out, rend the one possessed, and then leave the person. The person would fall down as dead but then rise later in victory and deliverance from the foul spirit. The highest compliment

I can give to the ministry of Brother Branham is that he showed to me, and millions more, that Jesus Christ is *"the same, yesterday, and today and forever!"*[461]

JESUS' COUNSEL TO BE CLOTHED

To conclude this book, my final thoughts come from the words of the Lord Jesus Christ from Revelation chapters two and three. Christ's red-letter words in Revelation include some of the most inspiring, prophetic, specific, and applicable words for us in the 21st century. In these seven addresses to seven Gentile cities, the Lord Jesus offers counsel, compliments, rebukes, consequences, and eternal rewards to the those in the churches.

The final letter of these seven letters, written to the church at Laodicea, has the most bitter denunciation recorded in Scripture. Jesus offered no compliment to this blind, miserable, wretched, and naked group due to their pride, arrogance, and avoidance of recognizing their true spiritual condition. The Laodiceans felt no need for more of God. They had no physical persecution, so their age was easier physically, as they did not have to be slain for their faith. But sadly, they were slain by their own lusts, as they let riches and worldly goods deceive them into a lukewarm, nauseating spiritual condition.[462] Any spiritually-minded person should be able to see that we are living in a modern Laodicean condition today. Most churches are richer than ever, with bigger buildings and programs than ever before, yet the supernatural power of the Holy Ghost is at its lowest ebb because they do not want more of the Word of God. Instead, they want material possessions.

For a moment, focus on Christ' words in Revelation 3:18: *"I counsel thee to buy of me gold tried in the fire, that thou mayest be rich; and white raiment, that thou mayest be clothed, and that the shame of thy nakedness do not appear; and anoint thine eyes with eyesalve, that thou mayest see."* Jesus said that repentant, faithful Christians need three things: gold, white raiment, and eye salve.

First, gold represents time-tested, unwavering faith.[463] Most church members do not live by faith, which is assurance in the unseen promises of the invisible God.[464] Church members often reject the commands of God, creating a state

---

461 Hebrews 13:8
462 1 Timothy 6:9, Revelation 3:16
463 1 Peter 1:7
464 2 Corinthians 4:18

of unbelief in their lives. Unbelief is the opposite of faith. When trials come, these unbelieving church members choose the path that leads to an easier life, for they love money, wealth, soft living, possessions, and big church buildings more than the Word of God. Their lives are lacking spiritual gold—unwavering faith and trust in the divine promises of God. Your life can be different, as you can obtain this unwavering, mature faith in the midst of your hardships by obeying all the Bible's commands.

Second, eye salve represents the anointing of the Holy Spirit to see or discern the absolute truth of God. Paul wrote that Christians have received the eye salve, or enlightened eyes when they understood God's calling and the inheritance for the saints.[465] Most church members are blind, following blind leaders according to Jesus Christ, for He said that few will be saved.[466] Modern Laodiceans follow churches that itch their ears and tell them what they want to hear, rather than what they need to hear.[467] Most church members cannot see or understand the Bible-truths that apply to their lives. They will quickly say that the commands of God do not apply to them and applied only to the believers who lived in the days of Paul and other apostles. The Lord Jesus Christ said the blessing of God is upon the eyes of those who can see and hear the Word, repent, and be converted.[468]

Last, white raiment represents the righteousness of Jesus Christ, which is a life of spiritual integrity that walks in obedience to the Spirit, and not the flesh.[469] Jesus said that most Laodicean-church members were naked—not clothed—with a Spirit-led life of integrity to the Bible. When true believers receive the baptism of the Holy Ghost, they are being "*endued*" or clothed in power to live a life of integrity in obedience to the Spirit.[470] Here are a few examples to show whether churches have kept Jesus' words with integrity:

- churches publish how much food and money they give to the poor, and yet Jesus taught not to let anyone know about how much we give to others.[471] Where is the integrity of secret giving?

---

465 Ephesians 1:18
466 Matthew 7:14, 15:14
467 2 Timothy 4:3
468 Matthew 13:15-16
469 Romans 8:4, Revelation 3:5, 19:8
470 Luke 24:49
471 Matthew 6:3-4

- church members frequently and willingly entertaining lustful thoughts, yet Christ said those who lust in their hearts are guilty of committing adultery.[472] How many millions of church members attend movie theaters on Saturday nights, enjoying sinful love-making scenes, murder scenes, and more evil—and then attend church on Sunday mornings without repenting, pretending they have Christian integrity? Where is the integrity of a clean mind and thought life?

- church members frequently use cuss words and even use God's name in vain. Where is the integrity of a bridled tongue? James 1:26 says, "*If any man among you seem to be religious, and bridleth not his tongue, but deceiveth his own heart, this man's religion is vain.*"

White raiment, then, has a deep spiritual meaning of godly integrity in obedience to the commands of Jesus Christ. Those without honest, Christian integrity are spiritually naked, devoid of all Christ's righteousness.

There is also a dual meaning for being clothed physically in God-honoring raiment that directly relates to this book, as Jesus said these Laodiceans were naked and unclothed. It cannot be coincidental that our generation is both the most spiritually naked and physically naked generation of all time. The history of American fashion contained in Chapter 6 fully proves this point. Never before in this nation's history have churches been full of members dressed in sexually-revealing fashions. Churches are full of women who flaunt shameful, bobbed haircuts. Churches are full of women lacking the shamefacedness that Paul commanded and instead their faces are painted like that of Jezebel. The counsel or advice of Jesus Christ is to be clothed both naturally and spiritually—with modest apparel and spiritual integrity.[473]

The only hope to be an overcomer in your day is to genuinely repent after receiving a rebuke from Jesus, Who is the Word of God.[474] As a true Christian, you should expect correction to come from the Word of God that you hear preached in God-fearing churches. This rebuke from Jesus, through His obedient preachers, is a clear sign of Jesus' love for His church, for God chastens every child of His that He loves.[475] If you and I can receive correction from the

---

472 Matthew 5:28
473 1 Timothy 2:9
474 John 1:1-3, 14, Revelation 19:13
475 Hebrews 12:6, Revelation 3:19

Word of God and zealously repent and change our minds and lives, we can be overcomers in this day and be granted the reward that Jesus promised—to sit with Him in His throne.[476]

Christ's counsel is to choose obedience. Choose modest clothes to cover the areas of your body that tempt others. Choose clothes that pertain to your gender. Choose a clean, makeup-free face and let it instead be lighted with the anointing of the Holy Spirit. Choose inexpensive and limited amounts of jewelry. Choose to keep your skin free from tattoo ink, punctures, piercings, and scars. Choose footwear that is flat. Choose the perfect will of God for your outward appearance through a transformed mind. Choose to be a part of God's plan to restore Christian modesty. Choose to make yourself ready for the return of the Lord Jesus Christ, for our Lord is coming for a wife that has made herself ready for her wedding day, according to Revelation 19:7:

> *"Let us be glad and rejoice, and give honour to him: for the marriage of the Lamb is come, and his wife hath made herself ready."*

---

[476] Revelation 3:21

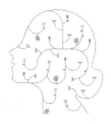

WORKS CITED

Ahmady, Amir, et al. "The Effect of Various Heights of High-heeled Shoes on Foot Arch Deformation: Finite Element Analysis." *National Center for Biotechnology Information*, www.ncbi.nlm.nih.gov/pmc/articles/PMC4101313/#!po=12.5000. Accessed 10 February 2018.

Al-Shawaf, Laith, et al. "Why Women Wear High Heels: Evolution, Lumbar Curvature, and Attractiveness." *National Center for Biotechnology Information*, www.ncbi.nlm.nih.gov/pmc/articles/PMC5693914/?report=classic. Accessed 10 February 2018.

"Baldness." *Encyclopedia Britannica*, www.britannica.com/science/baldness. Accessed 10 February 2018.

Burgess, Stanley, et al. *Dictionary of Pentecostal and Charismatic Movements*. Grand Rapids: Zondervan, 1998, pp. 372.

Beach, Stephen and Lindsey, Linda. *Sociology, 2nd Edition*. Prentice Hall, 2001.

Breining, Heather. "Ancient Hebrew Clothing." *Ancient Hebrew Research Center*, www.ancient-hebrew.org/culture_clothing.html. Web. 28 January 2018.

"Caitlyn Jenner." *Encyclopedia Britannica*, www.britannica.com/biography/Caitlyn-Jenner. Accessed 10 February 2018.

Collier's Encyclopedia. 1995, pp. 595.

Dictionary.com, www.dictionary.com/browse/modest. Accessed 10 February 2018.

Dorling Kindersley. *Smithsonian Fashion: The Definitive History of Costume and Style*. DK Publishing eBooks, 2012. Accessed 2 March 2013.

"Dress." *New Encyclopedia Britannica*. 1992, pp. 222.

English Oxford Living Dictionaries. www.en.oxforddictionaries.com/definition/legalism. Accessed 4 January 2018.

"Fashion and Dress." *Britannica Book of the Year*. Chicago: William Benton, 1970, pp. 341.

Goodstein, Laurie and Otterman, Sharon. "Catholic Priests Abused 1,000 Children in Pennsylvania, Report Says." *The New York Times*, www.nytimes.com/2018/08/14/us/catholic-church-sex-abuse-pennsylvania.html?action=click&module=RelatedCoverage&pgtype=Article&region=-Footer. Accessed 2 November 2018.

Gourley, Catherine. *Welcome to Molly's World, 1944: Growing up in World War Two America*. American Girl Publishing, 1999.

Greig, Cynthia and Catherine Smith. *Women in Pants: Manly Maidens, Cowgirls, and Other Renegades*. Harry N. Abrams, 2003.

Kopkowski, Cynthia. "Then and Now," *NEA Today Magazine*, September 2006.

L'Amour, Louis. *The Outlaws of Mesquite*. Random House Publishing Group, 1990.

Macy, Sue. *Wheels of Change: How Women Rode the Bicycle to Freedom (With a Few Flat Tires Along the Way)*. National Geographic, 2011.

"Mary Tyler Moore was the First Woman Ever on a Sitcom to Wear Pants." *Teen Vogue*, www.teenvogue.com. Accessed 17 January 2017.

"MeToo: A Timeline of Events." *Chicago Tribune*, www.chicagotribune.com. Accessed 25 December 2018.

Miller, Brandon Marie. *Dressed for the Occasion: What Americans Wore 1620-1970*. Minneapolis: Lerner Publications, 1999.

Murray, Maggie Pexton. *Changing Styles in Fashion: Who, What, Why*. Fairchild Books, 1989.

Packer, J.I. *Bible Almanac*. Nashville: Thomas Nelson, 1980.

Park, Madison. "Timeline: A Look at the Catholic Church's Sex Abuse Scandals." *CNN*, www.cnn.com/2017/06/29/world/timeline-catholic-church-sexual-abuse-scandals/index.html. Accessed 3 November 2018.

Pollard, Jeff. *Christian Modesty and the Public Undressing of America*. San Antonio: The Vision Forum Inc., 2004.

Rouse, Elizabeth. *Understanding Fashion*. Grafton Books, 1989.

Rubinstein, Ruth. *Dress Codes: Meanings and Messages in American Culture*. Westview Press, 1995.

The Holy Bible. King James Version, Holman Bible Publishers, 2012.

Time-Life. *The Roaring 20s: The Decade That Changed America*, 2017.

Voice of God Recordings, Inc. "The Bible: Hebrew and Greek Lexicons," *Voice of God Recordings*, www.branham.org/en/messagesearch. Accessed 10 February 2018.

Williamson, Ethel. "Short Hair, Long Career." *Reminisce Magazine*, January/February 1997.

"YouTube For Press." *YouTube*, www.youtube.com/yt/about/press. Accessed 5 June 2018.

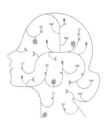

ACKNOWLEDGEMENTS

First, I give thanks to the Lord Jesus Christ for saving my soul and guiding me into all truth. Lord Jesus, You are my top priority and source of anything good that comes from my humble, little life. Without You, I can do nothing (John 15:5).

Many thanks to Isiah Brooks, Jon Gram, Brian Hawkins, Matt Leitner, and Keith Wilges for reading a chapter and providing feedback. Cam Smith, thank you for reading the entire book and being led by the Holy Spirit to make the largest doctrinal contributions to this text. Thanks to Mike McCloskey and Jon Gram for additional contributions to this project. Major thanks to Samuel Browning, Jim Shumake, and Simon Smith for reading the entire book and providing corrections and assurance. A big thank you goes to the members of Bride of Christ Fellowship for supporting this book in multiple ways.

To my editor, Joyce Greeley, a special thank you for your detailed, timely, honest, and straight-forward contributions you made to the manuscript. You were a true godsend and I'm very grateful for your investment in this project.

To my dear children, thank you for learning to love the Lord Jesus and creating such a wonderful home atmosphere. Your talents, letters, gifts, drawings, smiles, hugs, kisses, and encouraging words bless my soul. Your daddy loves you so very much.

Finally, to my wife, thank you for all your help and sacrifice that has allowed this book to become a reality. You inspired me to become an author after you wrote your first book. As you daily minister to our children and me, you support the reach of my humble ministry. I love you dearly, Kristen, as my eternal mate in glory.

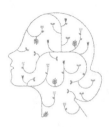

ABOUT THE AUTHOR

Jesse Smith is a bi-vocational pastor, also teaching public education in northeast Ohio. He helped establish Bride of Christ Fellowship in 2006 as its first and current pastor. To spread the gospel of Christ, Jesse preaches weekly to his congregation, helps teach two after-school Bible clubs, creates Christ-centered YouTube videos, and manages Brideofchristohio.com.

He's married to his high school sweetheart, Kristen. Together they shepherd their seven children.